CIA, INC.

CIA, INC.

ESPIONAGE AND THE CRAFT OF BUSINESS INTELLIGENCE

F. W. Rustmann, Jr.

BRASSEY'S, INC.
Washington, D.C.

Library of Congress Cataloging-in-Publication Data

Rustmann, F. W., Jr.
    CIA, Inc. : espionage and the craft of business intelligence / F. W. Rustmann, Jr.—1st ed.
        p. cm.
    Includes bibliographical references and index.
    ISBN 1-57488-388-7 (cloth)
    1. Business intelligence—United States. 2. United States. Central Intelligence Agency. I. Title: Espionage and the craft of busines intelligence. II. Title.

HD38.7 .R87 2002
658.4'7—dc21

                                                            2001052438

ISBN 1-57488-388-7 (alk. paper)

Printed in the United States of America on acid-free paper that meets the American National Standards Institute Z39-48 Standard.

CIA's Publications Review Board has reviewed the manuscript for this book to assist the author in eliminating classified information, and poses no security objection to its publication. This review, however, should not be construed as an official release of information, confirmation of its accuracy, or an endorsement of the author's views.

Brassey's, Inc.
22841 Quicksilver Drive
Dulles, Virginia 20166

First Edition

10 9 8 7 6 5 4 3 2 1

For
Fred Sr., Trey and Gabrielle, and Clayton H.
past, present, and future

THE MAN HE KILLED
by Thomas Hardy

Had he and I but met
By some old ancient inn,
We should have set us down to wet
Right many a nipperkin!

But ranged as infantry,
And staring face to face,
I shot at him as he at me,
And killed him in his place.

I shot him dead because—
Because he was my foe,
Just so: my foe of course he was;
That's clear enough; although

. . .

Yes; quaint and curious war is!
You shoot a fellow down
You'd treat, if met where any bar is,
Or help to half a crown.

Contents

Preface

Some of my former Central Intelligence Agency (CIA) colleagues will recognize a few of the operations described in the book and will note the deletions or changes I made to some of the names, locations, and other operational details. These changes were, of course, necessary to protect CIA sources and methods and other classified material. Under the terms of my employment with the CIA, the manuscript was reviewed by the agency's Publications Review Board to ensure that nothing described in the book would reveal secrets that needed to be kept classified. I found the review process to be fair, reasonable, and appropriate, and would like to take this opportunity to thank the board for its cooperation, understanding, and promptness during the review process.

Acknowledgments

would like to begin by thanking my wife, Teri, who encouraged me to write *CIA, Inc.,* and who then took up the slack in the office when I was busy working on it. The rest of the CTC group also deserves kudos for their technical assistance and indulgence during the writing process. A special note of gratitude goes out to Roy Jonkers and other members of the Association of Former Intelligence Officers; I drew heavily on the weekly intelligence notes and other AFIO publications for background and research material. Thanks also to Gil Dorland for introducing me to the Brassey's team; especially publisher Don McKeon and senior editor Don Jacobs, who believed in the book from the outset and carefully shepherded it through the editing and publication process. Finally, I would like to mention once again my appreciation to Scott Koch of the CIA's Publications Review Board for his scholarly, professional, and sensitive handling of the required CIA review process.

Introduction

SUN TZU AND THE ART
OF (BUSINESS) WAR

More than 2,500 years ago in China General Sun Tzu wrote *The Art of War*, a book that remains a classic on military tactics and strategy to this day. Even in those primitive years, Sun Tzu recognized the importance of possessing accurate intelligence to win. He devoted an entire section of his book to the employment of spies "to gather foreknowledge" of the enemy's condition and intentions—the type of information, he explained, that could not be obtained from spirits, gods, calculations, or comparison with past events; it could only be obtained from sources familiar with the enemy's situation. He called these secret agents "The Divine Skein." The treasure of a sovereign.

He divided these secret agents into five categories: native, inside, doubled, expendable, and living. Native agents referred to low-level penetrations of the enemy populace. Inside agents referred to higher-level penetrations of the enemy's government or military. Doubled agents were enemy spies turned back against the enemy. Expendable agents were people hired to spread fabricated information among the enemy. Living agents were people recruited to infiltrate the enemy's ranks and to return with information. Sun Tzu cherished his secret agents. He protected them and he rewarded them lavishly.

Things haven't changed very much over the years. Today, the CIA's clandestine service's main raison d'être is the recruitment and handling of foreign spies. In today's parlance, Sun Tzu's five agent categories would be termed low-level and high-level penetration agents, double agents, covert action agents, and access agents. Yes, things really haven't changed at all. After all, espionage is the second oldest profession.

Nothing is more valuable to our national defense than a well-placed penetration of an enemy government or military. Human spies can provide us with the intentions of an enemy; most technical forms of intelligence collection (satellites, overhead photography, communications intercepts, and so forth) can only tell us what the enemy is doing at the moment. Another step must be added to the process to seek intentions. It's called analysis.

Much of this book will be about human intelligence collection (called HUMINT in the trade). This is because HUMINT remains the most efficient, economical, and effective way to collect information. We will not, however, overlook other collection methods available to us. Things that were not available to Sun Tzu back in the Dark Ages.

Specifically, these methods include the use of open source information available on computer databases, the Internet, and elsewhere.

For business intelligence, the decade of the 1990s brought with it the advent of the personal computer, the related worldwide web, and the exponential spread of databases containing readily available, cheap information. Even in the government today, the problem is not the lack of information; it is the lack of qualified analysts and translators to put the information into usable form. There is a glut of information out there. This has made it possible to obtain information on individuals and companies, domestically and internationally, quickly and cheaply from a desktop PC. Only a few short years ago the collection of the same information would require hours of lugubrious effort rummaging through 3x5 cards in a library and days pounding the pavements in search of knowledgeable people to interview about a particular subject—a process so time intensive and expensive that most companies decided against any investigation at all. They just went with their gut feelings; they simply crossed their fingers and hoped for the best. There is no reason to do that today.

Think about it for a moment. Every major country on earth recognizes the need for intelligence and employs an intelligence service to collect it for them; every army on earth collects information on opposing forces and terrain, and they have done so since before the time of Sun Tzu.

It follows that businesses should do the same, particularly abroad where the terrain is less familiar, the rules of engagement are different, and the competition has the home-field advantage. Add to this the relative ease and economy with which this information can be gathered, and you've got a no-brainer.

Then why do so many companies continue to neglect this aspect of competition and try to wing it? Simply put, they are often reluctant to spend additional funds to collect information they think they can get by without. Sun Tzu would turn over in his grave.

The value of thorough, objective intelligence has been recognized since time immemorial; those who knew this fact were successful; those who didn't were losers.

Back in 500 B.C., Sun Tzu knew about the importance of collecting intelligence to know his enemy. The same thing applies in today's corporate world, where the importance of knowing the operating environment and the competition cannot be overstated. It's truly the key to success.

Part 1

BUSINESS INTELLIGENCE:
WHAT IT IS AND WHY WE NEED IT

1

THE CRAFT OF BUSINESS INTELLIGENCE

Sun Tzu was not just a bespectacled Chinese academician who spent all his time reading books and pontificating to the king's court about tactics and how to win battles. He was a hands-on combatant who rose to the rank of general by ruthlessly applying principles of warfare that he had devised over the years and set down in his book, *The Art of War.*

To give you an idea of the kind of man Sun Tzu was, one day about 2,500 years ago he was summoned by Ho Lu, the king of Wu. Ho Lu asked him rhetorically if he could train women in the same manner he trained men. Sun Tzu said he could, and King Ho Lu decided to test Sun Tzu. So he assigned 180 beautiful young women from the palace to Sun Tzu's army with instructions to teach them troop movement techniques.

Sun Tzu divided the women into two companies and placed the king's two favorite concubines in command of each company. Then he began to train them in the basics of close-order drill. He said, "When I give you the order 'Front,' face in the direction of your heart. When I give you the order 'Left,' face toward the left hand, and when I say 'Right,' face in the direction of your right hand. When I say 'Rear,' face in the direction of your backs." Sun Tzu went over all of this a few times to make sure everything was clear and asked them if they understood. They replied that they did.

He then called the two companies to attention and gave the command: "Face Right," and the women all burst into laughter. He settled the women down and said: "Okay, if my instructions were not clear, then it is my fault. Commanders must make sure their instructions are clear." So Sun Tzu repeated the orders three more times, explained them five more times, and asked if they now understood the commands. They replied that they did. Then he gave the command: "Face Left," and the women burst into laughter once again.

Sun Tzu settled them down again and said: "If instructions are not clear and commands not explicit, it is the commander's fault. But when they have been made clear and are not carried out, then the fault lies with the officers in charge of the companies." He then ordered that the two company commanders (the king's favorite concubines) be beheaded in front of their troops.

Sun Tzu didn't stand for any nonsense.

There were, of course, repercussions for Sun Tzu's actions; the king was not amused. Sun Tzu explained to the king that, as commander, his orders were final and admonished the king for trying to interfere with the tactical decisions of his commander. He then asked the king to watch him drill the two companies.

Sun Tzu selected two more women to lead the companies and began to drill the troops. He commanded them to face left, right, forward, and back, and so forth, and the women responded in strict accordance with the prescribed drill and not a giggle was heard from their ranks. He then told the king: "The troops are now in good order. They may be employed as the king desires, and they will even go through fire and water without a challenge to an order."

The king soon got over his pique, and Sun Tzu went on to win battle after battle for the Kingdom of Wu. He defeated the strong state of Ch'u to the west and subjugated the states of Ying, Ch'i, and Chin to the north. The Kingdom of Wu ruled supreme in that part of China for the next 100 years because of Sun Tzu's military achievements. And Sun Tzu's lessons are still being studied today by military and business leaders alike.

DEFEATING THE ENEMY

Business is war. Make no mistake about it. It may not be as bloody, but it is still a matter of survival of the fittest. The tactical lessons espoused by Sun Tzu so long ago are as applicable today as they were then, witnessed by the fact that the U.S. Marine Corps still requires every one of its officer candidates to read *The Art of War*.

To survive in today's cutthroat business environment, we must be properly armed. And one of the most important arrows in the businessman's quiver is accurate knowledge of his competitors and business environment—in other words, detailed knowledge of the enemy and the terrain of the battlefield.

Over 2,500 years ago Sun Tzu wrote: "If you know the enemy and know yourself, you need not fear the result of a hundred battles. If you know yourself but not the enemy, for every victory gained you will also suffer a defeat. If you know neither the enemy nor yourself, you will succumb in every battle." Frederick the Great also expressed his opinion on the importance of intelligence when he said: "It is pardonable to be defeated, but never surprised." In today's highly competitive business world, it is becoming more and more important to know your competition—know your enemy—and, particularly in the international arena, know your battlefield. There are minefields out there, and it is imperative to be able to identify and avoid them. As Sun Tzu pointed out, you can still lose, even when armed with superior forces, if the terrain is against you.

Possessing accurate intelligence is like having a flashlight in the dark. It won't remove any of the obstacles in your path, but it will illuminate them so you won't stumble.

BEING PREPARED

Realizing the importance of good, solid intelligence is the first step toward being prepared. The second step is employing experts to collect that intelligence. Some companies (AT&T, for example) have special competitive intelligence units within their organizational structure. Others hire professional consultants from outside of the organization to handle their intelligence-collection requirements or to augment their efforts. Either way, the craft of intelligence gathering and analysis is sufficiently arcane that it should be left to the experts. CIA case officers, for example, spend about a year at "the Farm," the CIA's covert training facility, attending formal intelligence training courses before being released to employ their skills abroad. Part of what they learn is how to collect information discreetly through the use of clandestine tradecraft methods, how to evaluate the sources of that information, and how to report that information accurately, objectively, and dispassionately. The Federal Bureau of Investigation (FBI) and some police departments also run intelligence-collection courses for their officers. The main difference between the CIA training and the FBI or police training is that the latter places more emphasis on techniques that use the power of the badge, while the CIA employs a more covert approach, relying more heavily on the use of cover and deniability to ensure a greater degree of discretion in its collection efforts.

Companies employing in-house resources often have difficulty obtaining objective information because of problems with training, resources, and vested interests. Company personnel are usually not trained in intelligence collection techniques, the companies usually do not have the requisite resources (computer databases, personal contacts, and so forth) to collect the information they need, and, finally, employees with a stake in the company's production will almost certainly lack the objectivity to report information accurately and without bias. The tendency is to paint pictures that support company policy or please superiors. This is precisely why professional intelligence consultants from outside the organization should be called in to handle the most sensitive intelligence-gathering missions.

WHAT IS BUSINESS INTELLIGENCE?

Generally, business intelligence can be broken down into three main categories: risk analysis, targeted collection, and counterintelligence.

Risk analysis is the assessment of general background information that a company needs to know to operate securely and effectively in an unfamiliar environment (usually international), where economic, political, criminal, insurgent, labor, or other forces could adversely affect a company's operations. This is usually multisource, analytical-type information. It is designed to prepare a company for all eventualities and to allow it to operate with "no surprises."

Targeted collection is a process by which specific information is gathered that the company can use to increase its productivity or market share. Market analysis; due diligence; background investigations on potential partners, employees, and others; and competitor intelligence fall into this category.

Counterintelligence is the process of gathering information meant to help protect a company's assets. This may sound unbelievable, but the White House estimates that the U.S. economy loses $100 billion (that's billion with a *b*) a year as a result of industrial espionage and the theft of proprietary information. And when proprietary information on a company's processes, patents, copyrights, products, and so forth is leaked, pirated, copied, or out-right stolen by a competitor, there is a compelling need to plug the leak and prosecute the offending parties. The purpose of counterintelligence is to collect information that will identify the spies within the company and the organization behind them and to provide enough evidence on the culprits to obtain convictions or press suits in a court of law.

We will discuss counterintelligence in greater detail in a later chapter devoted entirely to the subject.

RISK ANALYSIS IN ETHIOPIA

In the fall of 1990, I had barely unpacked my bags in Palm Beach when the phone rang. The call was from the Agency's Career Transition Center, a place through which many retiring CIA officers pass on their way out of the Agency womb and into private life; the center helps many employees find new lives after the Agency. The officer at the other end of the line explained that she had received a call from Maxus Energy, a Fortune 500 gas and oil exploration company based in Dallas, Texas. She explained that Maxus wanted to be put in contact with someone knowledgeable about Ethiopia. That's all they would tell her. Since I had served there as the CIA chief a few years earlier, she asked if it would be okay for her to give Maxus Energy my name and phone number. I said sure.

Shortly thereafter I was contacted by Maxus's director of corporate security, David Burton. David told me that Maxus Energy's petroleum engineers and geologists had found strong indications that significant reserves of gas and oil existed in the Ogaden region of Ethiopia, and they wanted to go there and look for themselves. The only problem was that no one in the company knew the first thing about Ethiopia; they were pretty sure there was oil there, but they didn't have a clue about the Ethiopian operating envi-ronment or the situation in the Ogaden (a very rough place at the time). This is where risk analysis enters the picture; research that points out the general obstacles to operating securely in the country.

The risk analysis report that I wrote for the company drew upon my past experience in the country and included multisource information derived from interviews with Ethiopian sources, computer databases, news archives, wire services, State Department databases and officials, economic publi-cations, and first-hand analysis. It covered the political situation (Was the current regime stable? If not, would a replacement regime honor previous commitments?), the economic situation (How stable was the Ethiopian birr? Could the local currency be moved out of the country freely? Should contracts be written in birr or U.S. dollars?), insurgency (What dangers would exploration teams face in the Ogaden? What type of security would be required to lessen the threat?), street crime (How should residences and equipment be protected?), and a general realities brief on the Ethiopian culture and people.

In short, the assessment provided Maxus's executives with a flashlight. It allowed them to move into a dark, unfamiliar area with few surprises. They knew what to expect, and they could now weigh the anticipated risks against the possible gains if they struck oil. They had the information they required to make informed decisions about the venture.

TARGET ON SOMALILAND

I worked with Maxus Energy for the next two years, providing them with a steady stream of information and guidance on how to work safely and securely in Ethiopia and, particularly, in the very dangerous Ogaden region. Then, one day about halfway through this period, I received a frantic call from David. He said Maxus's board of directors wanted to know if Maxus Energy could obtain drilling concessions in Northern Somalia, just over the Ogaden border from where they were currently exploring. He was quick to add that he was not interested in "the Mogadishu" Somalia; he wanted information on "Northern Somalia," a breakaway state with its capitol at Hargeysa that called itself the Somaliland Republic.

I was well aware of the problems that existed in Northern Somalia from my days in Ethiopia. The area known in colonial days as British Somaliland was in a state of total anarchy. It was waging an all-out war with the Mogadishu government, which opposed its secession, and tribal leaders were fighting an internecine war among themselves as they vied for positions of leadership and control. The government (what there was of one) couldn't collect sufficient taxes and therefore had little money to pay its army, let alone its public servants. And to make matters worse, the border region where Maxus wanted to explore was populated by bandits and littered with land mines left behind from years of border skirmishes. My risk assessment pointed out all of these facts. But despite the grim picture the assessment painted, Maxus decided to take the investigation a step further. The company wanted "targeted collection." It specifically wanted to know whether any drilling concessions were available along the Ethiopian/Ogaden border (they had heard that all concessions had been leased), and if so, could they obtain one and how much would it cost them.

This was information not readily available. Public records were scattered, incomplete, and in many cases, inaccurate. Access to them would require "bakhseesh" (bribes) to induce unpaid public servants to search for the records and the help of a high-level source within the government, preferably within the Ministry of Mining and Water, to obtain the information.

I sent the requirement to one of my Ethiopian sources and asked him if he knew anyone who could handle the request. He replied that a friend of his, an ethnic Somali from the port city of Berbera, had direct access to none other than the current minister of mining and water, Mohammed Ali Ateye. He said that Ali Ateye was a relative and that they both belonged to the Issaq tribe. This news was manna from heaven. He could answer all of our questions and had it in his power to make whatever arrangements we wanted. A meeting with Ali Ateye was subsequently arranged in neighboring Djibouti, and the two "access agents" took off from Addis Ababa on their mission.

They spent two days drinking, carousing, chewing khat (a mild native narcotic), and talking.

When they returned to Addis Ababa, they immediately contacted me and reported the results of their meetings with the minister. In short, as Maxus had suspected, the minister said most of the concessions had been leased to major oil companies, including Texaco, Conoco, Phillips, Chevron, Amoco, and Agip. He said these leases were nailed down and could not be broken. However, there was one lease held by a firm called Alliance Exploration, Inc., out of Alliance, Nebraska, that held a prime concession in the Burao region directly across the border from one of Maxus's Ethiopian exploration sites. He revealed that his agreement with Alliance Exploration could be broken because Alliance had failed to fulfill certain terms and conditions of the agreement. He added that he would agree to terminate the agreement in favor of Maxus Energy if Maxus was interested in picking it up. He indicated that Maxus would only have to pay "the going rate" for the concession, but the sources reported that a "commission" would have to be paid to Ali Ateye as well.

Armed with this information, the Maxus board reconvened to discuss the pros and cons of investing in the Somaliland Republic. They again considered the risks outlined in the risk assessment, and the cost (including an illegal bribe to a government official—something we will discuss at length in another chapter) and decided against the venture. I have no idea whether Maxus Energy now regrets that decision, but I do know it was based on the best information available to them at the time. Looking at the situation with the benefit of 20/20 hindsight, the deterioration of both Somali governments in the months and years that followed (Remember the fiasco of the U.S. military intervention there?) would seem to indicate that Maxus is still counting its blessings that it didn't charge headlong into that morass.

THE INTELLIGENCE PROCESS

Intelligence collection is a systematic process that requires excellent analytical skills and employs proven methods that ensure, to the extent possible, the accuracy of the information obtained. The process begins with a requirement. Within the U.S. government, intelligence collection requirements are generated by the White House, Pentagon, State, Justice, and other departments. In the business world, they are generated by company CEOs and other senior managers. These individuals usually know exactly what information they ought to have to ensure the trouble-free, efficient running of their businesses. They may also know where to look for unique business information that would give them the competitive edge they desire; they just do not know how to go about collecting it.

So the process begins with a question. Exactly what does the CEO want to know? This is the most important step in the process. It forces the CEO to analyze the problem and refine it from "I want to know everything there is to know about my competitor" to "What is my competitor's strategy to obtain the XYZ contract in Jakarta?" or "What plans does my competitor have to enter the widget market in Latin America?" Once the requirement is defined, the next step is to do a target analysis. In other words, to examine the competitor organization with an eye toward identifying where within the organization the information normally would be held (marketing department, research and development staff, legal department, and so forth). Once this is established, the scope is narrowed further to the individuals within the target department. They are then investigated and assessed to determine who would be the most knowledgeable and accessible source. Finally, when the target individual is selected, an operation is designed to extract the information from him or her. This usually requires the use of covert collection techniques, including elicitation, debriefing, the use of a suitable cover for the inquiries, and other overt methods, including database searches, interviews of other knowledgeable sources, and the like.

Thus, the intelligence process, whether in government or industry, involves four major steps:

1. defining the requirement;
2. collecting information on the requirement from all available overt sources (databases, library research, and so forth);
3. analyzing the overtly available information and organizing it into a cogent preliminary report on the subject;
4. identifying the gaps in the information and filling them through the use of more targeted covert collection techniques, and writing the final, comprehensive report.

This is the most efficient and efficacious approach to intelligence gathering and analysis. It is the technique used by the CIA and other government intelligence agencies, and it is the proper way for industry to collect business intelligence.

THE URGE TO WING IT

Managers who choose not to do their homework before they embark on a course of action are doomed to failure. Successful people always do their homework. Years ago when I was teaching the craft of intelligence to new CIA officers at the Farm, I discussed the concept of thorough preparation as the single most important key to success in the intelligence business. I explained that although all good operations officers certainly have the ability to wing it when necessary, the best officers never go into a situation with that intention. They try to prepare for every possible eventuality in advance, and then only have to improvise when a real unexpected curve is thrown at them. That's good advice for any business.

To quote Sun Tzu once again: "To remain in ignorance of the enemy's condition, simply because one grudges the outlay of a hundred ounces of silver . . . is the height of inhumanity." Perhaps it would be more accurate if the word *stupidity* were substituted for *inhumanity*. The military advice that Sun Tzu espoused so long ago applies equally to today's business. Know your own and your competitor's capabilities, and know your battlefield. Armed with this knowledge, you cannot lose—the worse thing that can happen is that you decide not to engage.

2

THE IMPORTANCE OF
INTELLIGENCE

The intelligence process starts with research, doing your homework, and collecting information on the subject to be researched. Then that information is collated, analyzed, and disseminated to whomever will act on it—the decision makers. Intelligence is not just raw information. It is evaluated information. No one should ever embark on a project without first researching it thoroughly and then putting all of that raw information to the analytical test of what's important and what's not so important, what's most likely correct and what's possibly wrong (usually depending on the sources of the information), and what logically fits and what doesn't.

EXAMPLES OF MISCUES

Why do we need business intelligence? Why do we need to research a project before jumping into it? Let's look at some egregious examples of mistakes that were made because the decision makers were either too lazy, or disinclined for whatever reason, to do a little basic research before they leaped.

Hong Kong Coins

During the mid-1970s, the Hong Kong government came out with a new fifty-cent coin. The problem was that it was about the same size, shape, and color as the existing twenty-cent coin, so people kept confusing the two. They bitched and complained and ridiculed the government loudly for making such a stupid mistake. People put dots of nail polish on the new coins to help distinguish them from the twenty-cent coins and raised such a stink that the coins were pulled out of circulation about a year later.

Dumb, right? A little basic research would have shown the Hong Kong government that other countries had experienced similar problems, and the mistake would have been avoided. This couldn't happen again, could it?

You guessed it! Those who don't study history are bound to repeat it. Only a few years later, the U.S. government issued the Susan B. Anthony silver dollar. Whoops! Looks and feels just like a quarter! Same mistake. Same reason behind it—nobody bothered to research the subject. Don't we ever learn?

The new U.S. dollar coin is an improvement, but it's still too close for comfort to the size and weight of a quarter. That's why you probably don't have any one-dollar coins in your pocket at this moment.

What's in a Name?

Remember the Chevy Nova story? General Motors couldn't sell the car in Puerto Rico or Latin America because *no va* means "does not go" in Spanish. The automobile was introduced back in the 1960s, and the story was well known in automotive circles. But that didn't stop Ford from naming not one, but three successive models without researching how the names translated into foreign languages. They were the Fiera, which means "ugly old woman" in Spanish; the Caliente (Comet), which is slang for "streetwalker" in Spanish; and the Pinto, which means "small male appendage" in Portuguese. Some people never learn! Nobody ever bothered to translate the name *back* from the foreign language *into* English before spending millions of dollars on marketing and shipment of the vehicles to foreign markets.

Muslims and Pork

The list of similar gaffes is endless. An American firm submitted a carefully detailed business proposal, expensively bound with a pigskin cover, to its Saudi Arabian potential client. Needless to say considering the Muslim religious taboos against pork and pork products, that deal never came off. And there is an old story about how England's East India Company lost control of India to the British Crown in 1857 partially because its Asian Indian soldiers refused to bite the tops off the bullets supplied to them. In those days the tops of the bullets, which were encased in pig wax, had to be bitten off before the bullets could be loaded and fired. The bullets were later modified, but too late to save the East India Company. (Note: Some historians will refute this story, but regardless of the truth, it is a good illustration of what could have happened.)

Broiled Sushi

More recently a large U.S. supermarket chain tried to impress its Japanese clients by serving sushi and tea. Unfortunately, the tea was Chinese, and the sushi was cooked!

What is it that drives people to plunge into costly projects without doing any preliminary basic research? Is it intellectual arrogance? Sheer stupidity? Or just incompetence? Why anyone would enter an unfamiliar dark room and choose not to use the light switch is beyond me. But some people do, and that's why they remain in the dark.

Successful people do their homework. The importance of intelligence cannot be understated. That's good advice for any business.

DO YOUR DUE DILIGENCE

While discussing the importance of research, I used the analogy of a person entering an unfamiliar dark room and *choosing* not to use the light switch. Not a very smart idea unless one enjoys bumping into furniture! To the businessman, a due diligence investigation is like that light switch—it illuminates the playing field. As I said earlier, it won't eliminate any of the obstacles, but it will show where they are so they can be avoided.

The following story presents a vivid example of why a company should never enter into a business deal without first doing a thorough due diligence investigation on the prospective partners. I have changed a few names and dates to protect some embarrassed parties and litigants, but the story is absolutely true.

For the first ten years of its existence, Rose Cosmetics enjoyed steady growth. By 1991, under the leadership of its founder and CEO, a bright, energetic entrepreneur named Rosen, the privately held company was grossing almost $50 million a year in sales of low-end perfumes and cosmetics. Then Mr. Rosen decided it was time to expand abroad.

He approached a British perfume supplier that he had dealt with extensively in the past. The company was run by a family belonging to an Indian sect that had been involved in the cosmetics trade in Europe and the Near East for many years. At first blush it appeared to be a good match for a partnership, so a deal was quickly struck. As part of the deal, the Indian family quietly acquired 65 percent of Rose Cosmetics stock. This fact, perhaps inadvertently, was not reported to the Securities and Exchange Commission (SEC) when the company was later taken public.

Following the Initial Public Offering (IPO), and due in large part to Mr. Rosen's excellent reputation in the industry, Rose Cosmetics stock began to take off. Then, bolstered by its further success in marketing a designer alternative line, the stock continued to rise astronomically until it reached a high of $28 a share by early 1993.

By this time, Mr. Rosen had voluntarily stepped down as CEO and had taken a backseat to the London-based Indian family in the running of the company. He contented himself with playing the options market with Rose stock and lending his creative expertise to the company until disaster struck.

When a *Forbes* magazine article announced that Rose Cosmetics was actually controlled by members of an Indian sect, and that the sect was reputedly involved in illegal black marketeering and money laundering activities, the stock plummeted. In a matter of weeks, it dove from $28 to $4 a share, and Mr. Rosen lost over $20 million in the options market. To make matters worse, the SEC launched an investigation that later resulted in federal indictments for a host of wrongdoings against Mr. Rosen and other former and current officers of the company.

Now, having lost his company and his fortune and facing prison, Mr. Rosen decided to check out his partners. He wanted to prove to the judge that the Indian owners were solely responsible for any illegal activities and the mismanagement of the company.

The due diligence investigation showed that the Indian family had indeed long been heavily involved, along with other members of the sect, in the black and gray markets for cosmetics as well as in illegal money laundering activities. It also showed that the new Indian CEO had twice been convicted of counterfeiting brand-name perfumes in the United Kingdom. In short, the London-based company and the Indian family had horrible reputations within the industry and a record of criminal conduct.

The due diligence report helped Mr. Rosen convince the judge that most of the guilt rested with his Indian partners. This information sufficed to keep him out of prison, but he still received some serious fines. This on top of his

$20 million stock loss and the loss of his company brought him to his knees. The Indians fared much worse.

Would Mr. Rosen have gone into business with the Indian family had he known about their nefarious past? Absolutely not. He deeply regrets not checking them out in advance. But that's what happens when one fails to use the light switch.

GAINING THE COMPETITIVE EDGE

By now, I don't think anyone will dispute the importance of possessing good intelligence before embarking on a venture, particularly a potentially risky one. Let's expand on that topic and discuss the best way to go about obtaining and evaluating information.

Remember the old *Dragnet* series, where Sergeant Friday used to knock on a door, flash his badge, and interrogate the occupant? "Just give me the facts, Ma'am," he would say, "just the facts."

That's how most police-trained investigators approach an investigation. They are used to having the power of the badge, and they tend to go directly for the jugular, often with less than subtle results. This is diametrically opposed to the way intelligence officers are trained to approach an investigation.

Intelligence officers rely more on guile than intimidation. The techniques of elicitation and debriefing are stressed over interrogation, and the use of tailored cover stories to collect information serves to enhance the accuracy of the information obtained. They are less likely to be lied to, or to be told what the interrogatees believe the interrogator wants to hear. For example, an intelligence officer posing as a doctor would be much more likely to elicit sensitive medical information from a subject than one posing as a plumber, but if one needed the plumbing plans to the subject's house, plumber cover would be ideal.

Employing cover has two distinct advantages: It puts the interviewee at ease and therefore makes them more willing to provide accurate, unbiased information—to reveal things they would not normally discuss with a stranger or a threatening interrogator—and the subject never knows the true reason for the questioning.

So the careful selection of cover to extract information from knowledgeable sources results in more accurate and fulsome reporting, while at the same time deflecting suspicion away from the real purpose of the investigation.

The Analytical Approach

Proper problem solving requires a precise analytical approach, and most investigations and intelligence-collection missions involve problem solving. In other words, most problems can be solved by obtaining the right information. If you are sick, the doctor first evaluates your condition by taking diagnostic tests, then decides what is wrong with you based on the test results, then prescribes a procedure to cure you of the illness.

In the intelligence profession, the trick is first to evaluate the problem and then to come up with a list of possible sources that possess the information desired (that is, who knows the answers to the questions, or what databases, files, and so forth contain that information). The next step is to target those potential sources and to devise appropriate cover stories to extract accurate information from each of them, or to find intermediaries who are sufficiently close to the target to ask the questions and to report the answers back to you accurately, fully, and dispassionately, without bias.

There are many subtle techniques used by professional intelligence officers to acquire information; they fall into the category of "clandestine tradecraft." Intelligence collection is vital to every investigation, and as I mentioned earlier, the art is sufficiently arcane that in most cases it should be left to the experts.

In-House Collection vs. Using Subcontractors

When a company's senior management comes to realize the importance of possessing good business intelligence, it must then decide how it is going to get that intelligence. There are essentially two ways: to use subcontractors—there are a number of reputable and capable business investigative firms out there, including CTC International Group, IGI, Kroll & Associates, Bishops Services, and DSFX, among others—or to create a business intelligence unit within the organization. The decision will depend on a number of factors, including the size of the company requiring the service, budgetary considerations, the amount of investigative support it requires, and the difficulty of acquiring the information sought.

A small or even medium-sized company with a limited budget would be foolish to invest in an in-house business intelligence unit. Depending on the industry, even a large Fortune 1000 company might not have enough investigative work to keep an intelligence unit busy and productive. These people must and should turn to a professional business intelligence contractor for their investigation needs.

Even large multinational companies with in-house security and intelligence staffs will at times be forced to turn to specialists for hard-to-acquire business intelligence or complicated litigation investigation support. With this said, some aggressive companies find it desirable to have an in-house business intelligence unit to perform most, if not all, of their investigative work. This is particularly true for those companies involved in highly competitive and rapidly changing technologies. These companies must have a steady stream of intelligence on their competitors just to keep current with the industry.

When a company makes the decision to create an in-house intelligence unit, it must consider a number of factors, including the costs involved and the professionals it must recruit to staff the unit.

The Business Intelligence Unit

The in-house business intelligence unit must, at a minimum, be composed of two separate branches: collection and analysis. The collection branch should be staffed with a case officer experienced in human collection techniques and a computer exploitation specialist to surf the Internet and run the various databases that would be required for overt information collection purposes. The analysis branch should be staffed with one or more trained intelligence analysts, or what is commonly referred to in the intelligence business as a "reports officer."

Unfortunately, the three disciplines can rarely be found in the same individual. The gregarious and manipulative case officer is the antithesis of the introspective and contemplative analyst/reports officer, and the computer specialist is in another class far removed from the first two. These are separate disciplines, different talents, and contrasting mind-sets. The three types will be examined later on in the book in chapters devoted to recruitment, analysis, and database research. The thing to remember is that these different types of people tend to think with different hemispheres of the brain. It is therefore extremely rare to find an officer competent in all three areas.

The Tools You Will Need

The case officer and the analyst only require basic office necessities like phone; fax; computer, with Internet access; and other office accoutrements that will aid them in collecting information, organizing it, and putting it into an acceptable report format for dissemination to the decision maker. Arming the computer specialist is another matter entirely.

Databases are the main tools of the computer specialist, and some of the best ones are restricted to private investigators, attorneys, law enforcement officers, and other licensed professionals. Subscriptions are usually required, and users are also charged by the minute of on-line time. This subject will be discussed in great detail in chapter six, "Computer Databases and the Internet," but suffice it to say that the best database subscriptions (Lexis/Nexis, Dialog, Autotrak, Dow Jones, Pacer, to name a few) are often expensive and difficult to operate efficiently and effectively.

Once the logistics are in place and the team is assembled, it would still be prudent to call in a qualified consultant to help train the people, select the right software programs and databases, and generally get the office up and running in a professional fashion.

WHY THE U.S. GOVERNMENT WON'T HELP

This all begs the question: If the collection of business intelligence is sufficiently arcane as to be left to the experts, and if the U.S. government (CIA, and so forth) is the principle expert in the field, why then won't the U.S. government collect it for U.S. industry? After all, other countries, friends and foes alike, have been aggressively involved in intelligence-gathering activities targeted against U.S. industry for many years as well as in sharing this intelligence with their own business community. Some of these foreign activities targeting the U.S. industrial/military complex have even crossed the line into illegal, state sponsored, economic espionage, with full-scale bugging of hotel rooms and airplane seats, theft and trespass, copying of files from laptop computers and briefcases, and other illegal practices. (The difference between industrial espionage and business intelligence gathering is that the former uses illegal collection methods while the latter does not.)

In fact, there has been considerable debate within the government, and the CIA in particular, on this very issue. It began in earnest back in the early 1990s, when the Soviet Union collapsed and it was thought that the CIA could be retooled away from Soviet collection activities to helping the failing U.S. economy with needed business intelligence. While debate on the subject continues to this day, there is very little chance that the U.S. government (particularly the CIA and the National Security Agency [NSA]) will ever get involved in the routine clandestine collection of business intelligence for U.S. industry.

The problem is that the very nature of clandestinely acquired information makes it classified—not for dissemination to the general public—because sensitive sources and collection methods must be protected. So, if the decision were made to collect business information and to disseminate it to companies outside of the intelligence community, to whom would the information be entrusted? Certainly not to all of the companies. But then which ones? And to whom within each company? Only the CEO's? Could we trust a profit-minded CEO not to disseminate important competitive intelligence information down to the rank and file for them to act upon it? Probably not.

There is also a strong argument against the idea of diverting scarce government intelligence-gathering resources away from the national defense to the private sector, and the ethical conundrum of asking CIA case officers to spy for IBM or AT&T rather than the White House or the Pentagon. Would these case officers be willing to risk their lives and the lives of their agents in the pursuit of wholly economic goals for private enterprise? I don't think many would.

This is not to say that the CIA and other law enforcement agencies will not fight to prevent illegal industrial espionage in this country, or that they will fail to alert a major company if they learn, inter alia, that some very unfair business practices (payment of bribes, and so forth) were hurting U.S. companies' chances to compete fairly in a particular country. Indeed, the ears of NSA are tuned to just these kinds of activities, and when they obtain evidence of unfair competition occurring, they will report it to the companies concerned for them to take appropriate action. In short, the U.S. intelligence services will sometimes help out on the defense side, but not with the offense.

This means that the U.S. government will not develop and fund a program to collect business intelligence for U.S. companies. Thus, if a U.S. company wants to collect information that will help it level the playing field and perhaps give it a competitive edge over a foreign company, it must use its own resources for that purpose.

Sadly, the proliferation of charlatans, crooks, and scam artists has become a fact of life in the 1990s. Outside U.S. borders, this danger is even more profound. Executives in countries lacking the laws, regulations, safeguards, and reporting requirements in place in the United States know that their

American counterparts all too often rely solely on limited information and luck when dealing with foreigners. Consequently, they are far more inclined to engage in misrepresentation and deception in their business dealings with Americans and other foreigners. This poses significant risks to the uninitiated, but the responsibility for mitigating those risks rests squarely on the shoulders of the investor.

Part 2

THE COLLECTION PROCESS

3

THE RECRUITMENT
OF SPIES

Now that we know what business intelligence is and why we need it, we arrive at the heart of the matter: How do we collect and evaluate it?

Information is collected in a variety of ways. The collection techniques most common to the intelligence community are through the use of human sources, research, and technical means. All are important and one does not preclude the need for any other, but if I had to choose only one, I wouldn't hesitate for a moment to pick human source collection as the standout favorite.

Why? Because from before the time of Sun Tzu, a well-placed spy has always been the most valuable asset of all. A human source can be tasked to collect specific information to fill specific intelligence requirements. And only a human source can provide information on an enemy's intentions. All other means, with the possible exception of research, which by definition can only provide historical information, simply suck up data they come into contact with. Signals and electronic collection devices pull out of the air only what they can reach; overhead photography takes pictures of wide areas of terrain. Both then require huge investments in sorting, interpretation, and analysis before being reported as finished intelligence. A well-placed spy, on the other hand, can be asked a question, and the answer will often stand on its own.

SPIES ANSWER QUESTIONS

During my first tour as a CIA case officer, I was assigned to Saigon and tasked with the recruitment of "legal travelers" to North Vietnam. Potential legal traveler agent candidates included third-country diplomats, businessmen, and others who had the ability to travel freely in and out of North Vietnam. Once recruited, these agents could be tasked with intelligence requirements in a safe haven before they traveled to the target area; then they would collect information during their visit to the restrictive North Vietnam; and then, once back in the safety of the free world, they would be thoroughly debriefed by a case officer and the resulting information would be sent back to CIA headquarters as field intelligence reports.

One of these legal travelers was a Saigon-based Middle Eastern diplomat whom I had recruited to provide information on his country's relations with North Vietnam. One of his regular duties was to act as a courier between his country's embassies in Hanoi and Saigon. He was considered a "vetted" asset based on the reliable information he had reported in the past and on his successful passing of a polygraph test.

During one of these frequent courier trips, he happened to be in Hanoi during the evening of an intensive B-52 raid over the city. One of the targets of the raid was the city's downtown electricity-generation plant, and the White House wanted to know if it had been hit. However, because of cloud cover over the city, our satellites and overhead photography could not provide confirmation. And for some reason, the White House wanted the answer immediately, if not sooner.

The requirement was simple: Were the lights on or off in downtown Hanoi during that evening?

When the agent returned to Saigon the following day, I watched him deplane, made eye contact with him, and then signaled him to follow me to a deserted location within the Tan San Nhut airport terminal where we could talk privately without being seen together. I asked him the question: "Did the lights go out in Hanoi last night?" He replied that they flickered, but did not go off. He added with wide eyes that he was, however, scared spitless by the "rolling thunder" of the nearby B-52 raid that shattered windows in his downtown hotel. "What were you guys trying to do last night," he asked, "kill me?"

My intelligence report was short: "According to a reliable observer who was in Hanoi during the evening of (date), electric power was essentially uninterrupted throughout the night in the central district of Hanoi." The White House had its answer only a few short hours after the requirement had been levied. The B-52s had missed their target. All of this was confirmed a few days later when the skies had cleared and satellite photos revealed the whole story of the air attack.

INTELLIGENCE REPORTS

Intelligence reports from vetted agents in the field contain evaluated information. That's what makes them "intelligence reports" rather than "information reports." Intelligence is not just information. It is evaluated information. The source of the information (in this case the agent) is evaluated and weight is given to the report depending upon the degree of access the agent had to the information and the agent's reliability track record and successful completion of other testing and vetting methods (for example, the polygraph).

Did the agent see or hear the information with his own eyes or ears as in the Hanoi bombing case, or did he obtain the information through an intermediary. In other words, what was the agent's access? How reliable has the agent's past reporting been? Is she always truthful? Does he tend to exaggerate? Is he a keen observer? How good is her memory?

Finished intelligence is the final product of a process that involves the collection of raw intelligence, analysis of that information, and finally, the reporting and dissemination of the finished product to a consumer. In the trade, we call this the "intelligence process": collection, analysis, reporting, and dissemination of information. We'll discuss this in greater depth later on in the chapter on analysis.

THE CASE OFFICER

Before we get into the actual agent recruitment process, I should explain a bit about the title given to those intelligence officers who are responsible for human clandestine collection: the case officer. In the CIA, he or she is an intelligence officer attached to the operational (clandestine) arm of the Agency. The case officer typically is a college graduate, fluent in one or more foreign languages, and always a fully trusted American citizen with a Top Secret security clearance. He or she is an individual of exceptional intelligence, integrity, and initiative. The case officer "handles" operational cases; that is, the officer recruits and directs foreign indigenous spies who are known as "agents." The case officer is not an "agent"—the FBI's staff operatives are known as field agents; the CIA's (and other intelligence services) are known as case officers.

Few people ever get close enough to the Agency to know what a case officer is; so much fiction of the "James Bond" type distorts the truth and misleads the public about these unique individuals. Case officers are the Agency's elite corps, and they will remain so for as long as there is a need for human agents deep within foreign governments to provide our policy makers with intelligence information concerning foreign intentions toward the United States.

THE USE OF COVER

In addition to recruiting and handling agents, the case officer is trained in the use of cover to obtain information directly from sources through elicitation, debriefing, and other means. The trained case officer can become just about anyone he wants to be to get the information he needs. He is like a chameleon, changing his colors to suit any operational occasion.

CIA case officers work under two distinct types of cover when they are in the field: cover for *status* and cover for *action*. Cover for status is the cover that provides the case officer with the legitimacy to work in a particular foreign country. Obviously, the case officer cannot declare that he or she is in a country to spy on it, so the case officer is given a cover for status. In most cases, this cover is something official, usually a diplomat or a civilian official of the Department of Defense. In official cover situations, the case officer usually works out of a U.S. official military or civilian installation abroad.

The case officer may also be assigned abroad as a businessman or as a student or in some other nonofficial capacity. These case officers are called NOCs, nonofficial covered case officers. Like the officially covered case officers, the main reason for the cover is to give them a legitimate reason to live and work in the foreign country.

When either the NOCs or the officially covered case officers need a deeper cover to perform their operational duties, they take on an additional layer of cover: cover for action. Here they are usually in alias and have a totally different identity from their official or nonofficial cover. They may be of a different nationality (with documents to support the foreign citizenship), and any profession that suits their needs (businessman, journalist, academician, foreign diplomat, and so forth). These covers are usually lightly backstopped to one degree or another with a business address, phone number, and cover legend that can be verified by a less than thorough inquiry.

In my CIA career, I often posed as Harry McReilly, a rich and friendly Irish businessman; François du Bois, an equally rich and friendly French businessman; Fred Ryland, a stringer for this or that journal; Clayton Maxwell, a befuddled tourist; and a slew of other identities to suit almost any situation.

All I would have to do was walk out of my office, zigzag around the city a bit to shake any possible surveillance, then go to a local safehouse, where I would switch documents, change clothes, and emerge as Harry McReilly, François du Bois, Clayton Maxwell, or whomever.

THE RECRUITMENT PROCESS

The recruitment of new agent sources is the main task of the CIA case officer. Accordingly, one of the most important courses taught to new operations officers at the Farm, the CIA's covert training facility in Virginia, is "The Recruitment Cycle." It's a basic "how-to" course describing the steps and techniques required to induce the in-place defection of new sources of intelligence. The recruitment cycle involves four distinct phases: spotting, assessing, developing, and delivering the final recruitment pitch.

In short, the course teaches the new officers how to *spot* new agent talent (that is, find people with access to the information desired); how to *assess* their susceptibility to recruitment; how to use their perceived susceptibilities, vulnerabilities, and desires to massage and *develop* them to the point of recruitment; and then how to design and *deliver* a recruitment pitch based on the personal information obtained. Inducements of money, recognition, and revenge are examples of major motivators; most spies accept recruitment to gain one or more of these things.

RECRUITING YURI

The CIA course on recruitment includes a five-week-long practical exercise that is designed to take the students through the entire cycle in a realistic setting. In the first week, the students, who are all ostensibly assigned to a fictitious CIA station abroad, receive a cable from CIA headquarters announcing the arrival of a new diplomat from a country hostile to the United States. The cable provides a brief history of the target's (let's call him Yuri) previous foreign assignments, biographic data, any available assessment data that may have been picked up at earlier posts, and a physical description. The student meets with his chief of station, who instructs him to make contact with the target at the earliest opportunity and to assess him for possible recruitment. As the script plays out, the student learns that Yuri will be attending a cocktail party at another (neutral) foreign embassy to celebrate that country's national day.

At the cocktail party, the student spots Yuri and engages him in conversation. The student then tries to develop rapport and to elicit information from the target that will identify mutual interests that can be used for continuing the contact. In other words, what are Yuri's hobbies, favorite restaurants, sports, weekend pursuits? Is he married? Does he have children? All of this information is then used by the student to come up with a reason for the two to get together during week three of the exercise. Let's say Yuri admits to being an avid fisherman or tennis player. The student will invite Yuri to a tennis game or to fish; that is, if the student can play tennis or knows anything about fishing. If Yuri likes to play chess, a chess game may be the next step. Whatever mutual interest the student can identify will be the hook for the next contact.

During the third week, the assessment moves into high gear. This meeting permits the student to establish a firm foundation of rapport with Yuri and to use it to elicit information about Yuri's financial situation (Is he in need of money?), career (Is he moving up? Does he hate his supervisor?), family (Is he happy in his marriage? Does he regret not having the opportunity to educate his children abroad?), and anything else in his character that could be used to develop a recruitment pitch. Let's say Yuri admits to being continually passed over for promotion to first secretary and being stuck in a thankless job. Perhaps he also drops hints about a secret admiration for the West and a desire to educate his son at UCLA in California.

These bits of information will be used in the fourth week to develop Yuri toward eventual recruitment. In other words, the student will attempt to exacerbate Yuri's feelings of failure and desire and begin to plant ideas about how he could obtain the recognition he thinks he deserves while at the same time being able to afford to send his son to UCLA when the time comes.

In the final week, the student constructs and delivers a recruitment pitch designed to address all of Yuri's issues and to offer clear, obtainable solutions. Other things that will allow Yuri to rationalize his behavior (after all, he's about to be asked to betray his country) will be thrown into the pitch. Things like: "By helping the United States understand your country better, you will be contributing to world peace," and "Your country's political system is rotten anyway, and you're not the only patriot to take action to change it."

In addition to the rationalizations, Yuri will be offered the recognition he craves (albeit in the secret world of CIA "patriots"), money in a secret bank account that can be used for the later education of his son at UCLA (and whatever else he wants to use it for), and perhaps eventual relocation to the United States for him and his family after several years of dedicated service to the CIA. All this in return for whatever classified information he is able to obtain during the normal course of his diplomatic duties.

WHEN DIRECT ACCESS ISN'T POSSIBLE

When, for one reason or another, a case officer can't develop the proper cover to allow direct contact with a potential agent recruit (for example, a terrorist target), the case officer must step back and work through intermediaries, or access agents, as they are called in the trade (recall that Sun Tzu called them *living* agents).

An access agent is one who bridges the gap between the target and the case officer. He or she is a person who has natural cover to contact the target in a nonthreatening way. An access agent is usually an indigenous resident of the country where the operation is taking place, or the same nationality as the target. A person with whom the target is comfortable. Once recruited, the access agent is directed by the case officer to spot, assess, and develop potential recruits with direct access to the information desired. In the best of circumstances, the access agent becomes a confidant of the target; someone who can tweak the target's susceptibilities and develop them into recruitment benefits.

TARGETING

Agent candidates possessing accurate knowledge of the internal workings of the target abound. They are found within the walls of the target (penetration agents), or outside of the walls with the ability to walk in and out, or they are people on the outside who have direct access to people who are on the inside (access agents).

The first step is to analyze the problem. Where within the organization would the desired information be held? The production department, marketing, legal, human resources? Then, who in the target department would be the one most likely to provide the information? An underpaid secretary, disgruntled junior officer, alcoholic blabbermouth senior vice president? You get the idea. Whether the target is a foreign embassy or a competing company, the targeting process is the same.

PENETRATION AGENTS

Once you have spotted the individual you want to target for recruitment, you go after him or her and continue with the recruitment cycle: direct assessment, development, and recruitment. The penetration agent is the best asset for this, because, once recruited, he can provide a continuing stream of information for as long as he is with the target. But he is also the most difficult and costly (in terms of time and money) to acquire. Most companies would not have the patience, budget, or inclination (we're getting into the area of corporate espionage here) to run penetration operations the way the CIA does. But some foreign governments bent upon obtaining a U.S. company's proprietary secrets certainly would, and frequently do.

A COSTLY AND TIME-CONSUMING ENDEAVOR

Let me give you a feel for what I mean. When I was stationed in East Asia, a cable arrived from CIA headquarters directing me to assist another Asian station with a particularly difficult but high-priority recruitment effort. The target was a third world communicator, a code clerk. (Let's call him Nabil.) Although relatively low on the embassy totem pole, he had access to his country's encryption codes as well as the ability to read every piece of official traffic, classified and unclassified, that went through his embassy. Nabil was a tough revolutionary who had fought in the trenches and back alleys to throw the Imperialists out of his country, and he bore the scars to prove it: a jagged shrapnel gash on his cheek and an ugly, dimpled bullet wound through his right biceps. He spoke neither English nor the local language and hated all Americans and most other foreigners.

The station had direct access to him through one of its French-speaking NOC officers, but the station was afraid to risk blowing the NOC's cover in a chancy recruitment effort. It was equally afraid of risking any of its officially covered officers, because a botched operation could result in the identification and expulsion (declaring an officer persona non grata) of the case officer. So CIA headquarters and the station decided that an outside case officer under deep, nonofficial cover should be used to approach the target, and I was the guy they picked.

After studying the case file, I boarded a plane for the first of what would turn out to be a dozen trips back and forth between my home station and the country where the target was assigned. A station case officer assigned in the country met me at the airport and briefed me on the case during the drive into the city. Later that evening, after checking into a hotel under the alias Harry McReilly (the rich and friendly Irish businessman), I met with the NOC officer and the inside case officer in a downtown safehouse. Together we devised a plan to contact Nabil without any direct involvement of any station assets.

The NOC officer provided me with several interesting and actionable pieces of information to use in my initial approach. First, because of his language limitations (very little English), the target's social circle was limited to his embassy colleagues and a few local French-speaking friends. Second, he fancied himself to be quite the ladies' man and spent all of his money and free time in a local gin mill trolling for local prostitutes with whom he communicated in bar-girl pidgin English. Last, the NOC related that among Nabil's closest friends in the country (outside of his embassy cohorts) was a French couple who were in the process of being reassigned back to Paris.

Most important, the couple's house was being advertised for rent. This would provide an excellent opportunity for me to meet them face-to-face before their departure.

Armed with this information, I found an ad for the house they were vacating in a local newspaper and called the real estate agent to make an appointment to see it. I arrived at the property while the French couple was busy packing out. I introduced myself as Harry McReilly and went to work trying to use my (Irish) charm on them. We spoke French together and quickly established rapport. I played the new guy in town and they happily gave me tips on local living conditions, where the best French restaurants were, what to do and not to do, and so on. I met their dog and their maid and their neighbors and generally became familiar with them and their surroundings. With this operational groundwork accomplished, I left the country and returned home to wait for them to leave the country.

About two weeks later, after the station had confirmed that the French couple had departed, I returned to the country, checked back into the hotel as McReilly, and phoned my target at his embassy. Because I didn't want to leave a message and he was always either out of the office or otherwise unavailable, it took me two days before I could get him on the line.

I introduced myself as a friend of his French friends and told him that I had visited them recently during my only previous trip to the city and that I had just run into them in Paris. I said they had suggested I give him a call when I got to town and added that our mutual friends seemed to believe we had a lot in common and should get together. I established my bona fides by casually slipping in comments about the couples' appearance, their house, their dog, the maid, and so on. Nabil was cautious at first but finally accepted my cover story and agreed to meet in his favorite bar the following evening.

I got to the bar a few minutes early and waited for more than two hours buying drinks for the bar girls, chatting with the bartender, and drinking on an empty stomach. But the target never showed up. I was stood up. Such is the life of a case officer.

I called him the following morning and was told that he would not be on duty until late that afternoon. So I cooled my heels another day in the city and called him early that evening. Nabil explained, without apology, that something else had come up at the last minute. When I tried to reschedule, he explained that he would be working nights for the rest of the week but suggested having a lunch together the next day beside the pool at one of the major hotels in town, another one of his regular haunts. We described each other and agreed to meet at noon at the poolside bar.

He was not hard to spot at the pool; tall, thin, classic Middle Eastern features, bikini bathing suit, and, of course, those scars. I approached him and introduced myself. We sat at a table overlooking the pool and ate lunch while we talked about our mutual friends and life in the city (especially the night-life) and generally established rapport. Knowing that he would not be able to get out over the next few days, I told him I had to leave the following day but would be returning in a week or two. This allowed me to elicit information about his work schedule and to plan my return around it. I flashed a lot of cash; paid for lunch, leaving an exorbitant tip; and teased him with the prospect of having a rich, nonthreatening friend who would cruise the bars, restaurants, and nightspots with him and, of course, would pick up all the tabs. The hook was in, and now it was up to me to play the line carefully so that I could eventually reel him in. This was a very big fish indeed, but he would be a difficult recruitment target.

I made about ten more trips back and forth between the two cities over the next four months. Rapport and trust grew with each visit. We dined, drank, and caroused together. I picked up all of the bills, never forgot to bring him gifts of scotch or cognac from the airport duty-free shop, and usually paid for his women as well.

I had assessed my target as a venal, sexual Walter Mitty. He fancied himself quite the Don Juan with the local hookers and didn't seem to get it that it was his money, and not his good looks and charm, that kept the girls jumping in and out of his bed. It was also an expensive habit, one that put a severe strain on his meager monthly salary. And as he became more and more dependent on his friend McReilly to support his carefree, playboy lifestyle, I started going for the quid pro quo.

I began nonthreateningly by asking for his advice concerning general investment opportunities in the Middle East and then started focusing him on the petroleum industry. As a member of the Organization of Petroleum Exporting Countries (OPEC), his country was privy to private talks among the members concerning pricing, quotas, and the like. These were rather benign intelligence requirements to start with, but frankly, I didn't care if he gave me nursery rhymes at this stage. All I wanted to do was to get him in the habit of giving me something for which I could give him something in return. Once this routine was established, and Nabil became comfortable with discussing borderline secrets with me, I began upping the ante, and formalizing the quid pro quo relationship.

I did this by asking him to collect overt information on petroleum trade policies during my absences from the city, and then briefing me on them during my visits. The briefings gave me the opportunity to elicit additional information on the subjects that Nabil had access to through his job as a code clerk in his embassy. Minor intelligence reports began to trickle back to CIA headquarters as a result of these debriefing sessions. But most important, since he was providing me with this "press clipping" service, I was able to offer him a regular monthly stipend for his efforts. The stipend, which was paid in cash, not coincidentally roughly equaled his monthly government salary.

Nabil was now providing information on sensitive topics in return for money. The hook was definitely in. And as he became more and more comfortable talking to me and more and more reliant on the money, I began reeling him in. The topics we discussed became more and more sensitive, and the debriefing sessions became longer, more detailed, and more businesslike.

Eventually, he was developed into a fully recruited source with full knowledge that the end user of the information he was providing was the U.S.

government. At this point, I turned him over to an inside station case officer for clandestine handling.

Because of the Agency's "need to know" policy—the policy that each officer is only given the information they need to know to perform their specific tasks so that projects and sources aren't compromised—I was removed from the picture at this point and was given no more information on the case. Corridor scuttlebutt, however, indicated that he was a long and productive asset of the CIA.

INTELLIGENCE HUMOR

In closing this chapter on the recruitment of spies, I would like to pass on some apropos humor currently circulating in the halls of the intelligence community in Washington, D.C.

There was an IMINT guy, a SIGINT guy, and a MASINT guy sitting together in a bar. (For those of you who are not familiar with these intelligence disciplines, IMINT is imagery intelligence, SIGINT is signals intelligence, and MASINT is measurements and signatures intelligence.) They were having a chat, and they noticed a couple of young ladies sitting on the other side of the room in a corner and having a very heated discussion. The guys looked at each other and said: "It would be really nice if we knew what those young ladies are saying. We're all intelligence types, so we should be able to figure this out."

The IMINT guy pulls out a big telescope and says: "I can do it. I've got this new imaging system with a new focal-point array that I can update very rapidly. I can then look at the video, read their lips, and figure out what they're saying." He sets it up, gets it calibrated, and gets it in focus. But every time it's properly focused, the ladies turn and he can't see their lips. He mutters something about terrain masking and says, "I can't do it."

The SIGINT guy says, "I've got it! I've got this new joint SIGINT avionics family. It's the latest digital system for the Department of Defense." He pulls it out and says, "I've got the whole spectrum digitized. I can focus in on what they're saying and figure out what they're discussing." He tunes it up and at first gets a conversation over on the other side of the bar, a couple of gentlemen discussing business. He keeps tuning and tuning but only gets an FM radio station with loud rock-and-roll stuff. He can't hear what the ladies are saying, and he mutters something about cochannel interference and says, "I can't do it."

The MASINT guy says, "I've got it! I've got this great new technique where I use lasers to illuminate the subjects, and then with a hyperspectral detector I can figure out the acoustic modulation of the salinity content of the sweat on their brow, and by that I can figure out what they're discussing." He gets it all set up and tuned in and data comes spewing out of the system; tons and tons of data. But he doesn't seem to be getting any signatures, and he mutters something about aerosol scattering in the cigarette smoke and he admits, "I can't do it."

So they had pretty much given up on figuring out what the young ladies were discussing, when the ladies come over and say: "We understand you were trying to figure out what we were discussing."

The intel guys look at each other, sorely puzzled, and the ladies say, "What we really ended up discussing was whether or not you guys would ever figure out what we were talking about."

The IMINT guy says: "Well, yeah, we were. But how did you know that?" And one of the young ladies says, "Well, we just tipped the bartender ten bucks and he told us. It's called HUMINT, human intelligence."

4

ALTERNATIVES TO
RECRUITMENT

Recruitment operations are the bread and butter of any intelligence organization. There is no better way to obtain information on a target than to have a well-placed penetration agent deep within its infrastructure. The penetration agent can provide historical information as well as regular intelligence updates and future plans. The problem is that these operations are difficult to orchestrate, expensive, and can't be planned and executed overnight. They require enormous resources and patience. Also, if the information obtained is proprietary (and it usually is), obtaining it is illegal; the spy is essentially stealing from the target company, and in many states, the case officer can also be accused of being an accessory to the theft.

We will be discussing these legal issues in greater depth later on in the book, but the important thing to know is that these techniques exist and can be used against you by U.S. competitors or foreign companies. In the latter case, the foreign companies often act with the full consent (and sometimes collusion) of their governments, giving them a degree of protection from any legal action that could be directed against them.

DEFECTORS

One of the most popular ways to obtain intelligence on a company or country is to induce (or simply accept) the defection of one of its officers. By definition defectors can only provide historical information, but this can still be extremely valuable. Important defectors are debriefed by the CIA over periods of months or even years and are often compensated richly in the form of healthy salaries or annuities, resettlement in the United States or another friendly country, living expenses, and expensive homes. They are also sometimes given new identities and secret offshore bank accounts to hide their newfound wealth and to shield them from retribution from their previous government.

The experience is not so different in the private sector. Engineers, designers, technicians, systems managers, and senior officers often play musical chairs jockeying for jobs among competing companies in similar industries. These individuals leave their previous companies with their heads full of proprietary information on the designs, formulas, sales projections, and plans of their old company. Despite noncompete agreements and written warnings that confidential information not be divulged to a new employer, the information they possess cannot be mysteriously erased from their brains when they leave one company and begin working for a new one. Companies realize this and just deal with it. They have no other choice.

Despite the clear and growing threat of foreigners stealing U.S. trade secrets, the real problem is right here within the United States. Company insiders are responsible for a much greater percentage of theft than foreigners, and the primary motives for betrayal are the same for this group as for anyone else committing espionage: money, revenge, and ego. Also, the main reason for trade secret theft in the United States today is the disparity in income between relatively low-paid product designers and the top managers. Bosses are often paid enormous salaries and offered lucrative stock options, and this causes resentment among the engineers in the ranks. They feel shortchanged, and this often leads them to rationalize their actions when they steal secrets from one company to sell to another.

But it is only when one of these employees leaves with the blatant intention of bringing classified information from one company to another, usually in the form of boxes of documents or computer disks full of plans and formulas, that they cross the line and possibly subject themselves to prosecution under the Uniform Trade Secrets Act.

Xerox Corporation engaged in a bitter dispute with IBM over this issue a few years ago, and more recently General Motors (GM) accused Volkswagen (VW) of blatant industrial espionage in a much publicized case involving the hiring of GM officers who not only brought their knowledge from GM to VW, but also purloined boxes of files containing reams of confidential trade secrets. The case is a classic example of one company's aggressive attack against another to gain market share in a highly competitive industry.

GM VS. VW

By the early 1990s, Jose Ignacio "Inaki" Lopez had established himself as a shaker and mover within GM's ranks. He had been instrumental in saving GM more than $1 billion in supplier costs and revolutionizing the way cars are assembled and was on his way to being promoted from vice president of purchasing to president of North American operations. Then, in March 1993, he suddenly quit GM, along with a half-dozen of his closest aides, to become a top VW executive for a salary of $1.6 million a year—nearly five times what he earned at GM, and well beyond the norm for executive compensation in Germany. His defection was unparalleled in the history of corporate America, and it resulted in a massive civil lawsuit being filed by GM against VW. The suit alleged that the mass defection was part of a plot by VW to steal GM trade secrets. And from all appearances, that's exactly what it was.

A close reading of the case indicates that VW's chairman, Ferdinand Piech, personally orchestrated the defection during a six-month-long development of Lopez. The case is a classic example of an induced defection for industrial espionage purposes.

Piech probably initially spotted Lopez in the early 1990s when Lopez was GM's managing director for its European operations. At the time, Piech was interested in obtaining information on new product plans for Adam Opel AG, GM's European subsidiary and VW's most dangerous competitor. Once Piech had set his sights on Lopez, he ran a textbook recruitment operation to induce his defection. He clearly knew that an induced defection brought with it the advantage of having a recruited source within GM for at least a short time—long enough to direct his new agent(s) to amass a fortune in classified documents before actually jumping ship.

Piech's development of Lopez followed an assessment period that included, among other things, a psychological evaluation of Lopez to determine his vulnerabilities, susceptibilities, character, temperament, and career aspirations. Armed with this assessment, Piech arranged a personal meeting with Lopez at the Detroit area headquarters of VW. He clearly touched the right buttons, because his discussions with Lopez were orchestrated to show that the two had many similar likes and dislikes. That initial meeting was followed up with several additional get-togethers and numerous phone conversations over the next two months. An aura of rapport and trust was firmly established during this development period, and both professional respect and a friendship resulted.

Following the favorable assessment and an approximate three-month-long development, Piech delivered his recruitment pitch to Lopez. He offered money and corporate power in return for GM's most tightly held secrets. And, since the pitch came several months before the actual defection took place, Piech could begin tasking Lopez while he was still inside GM. Lopez was directed to begin collecting and assembling information of intelligence value and, on the operational side, with arranging the similar defections of his six cohorts.

One of these defecting aides was Jorge Alvarez, who was privy to all of the confidential information relating to the development of Opel's new cars that would compete with VW in Europe. Another was Andre Versteeg, who was working on a top secret car development project at Opel in Germany. Other information Lopez was tasked to obtain included details of a highly confidential cost study of a proposed factory of the future, a project known within GM as "Plant X."

As in a cold war espionage operation, the assembling of the stolen data and its removal from GM's premises was accomplished using clandestine techniques right out of a spy novel. Using the name of another Opel employee to cover his tracks, Versteeg mailed a box of confidential documents to himself in the United States. Meanwhile, Lopez obtained the only two existing copies of the secret "Plant X" document from its author, Manfred Schonleber, Opel's purchasing executive. He then kept one copy for himself and sent the other to Jose Gutierrez, another top aide who joined him in the defection. On the day of his departure from the United States, while Lopez and his family were arriving at VW's headquarters in Germany, a VW corporate jet landed in Barcelona to pick up twenty cartons of GM documents that Lopez and his aides had sent to the home of Lopez's brother-in-law in Spain. Another sixty-five-pound box of documents was shipped from VW's U.S. headquarters to VW in Germany a few days later.

Within a week of Lopez's defection, his six "warriors," as he called them, resigned from GM to join him in Germany. Things were indeed very grim at GM. A search of Lopez's office revealed that documents containing some of the company's most sensitive secrets were missing. Then, armed with a list of documents Lopez or his aides had requested from various GM offices during the previous couple of months, they found that only a few remained. Similar searches of the aides' offices found none of the missing documents.

Over the next month, the purloined documents were copied into VW's computers. Once this task was accomplished, two of Lopez's aides moved all of the original documents out of the VW premises and brought them, along with a heavy-duty shredder, to a hotel room near VW's Kassel plant. They then spent the better part of the next three days destroying the evidence.

Unfortunately for Lopez and his accomplices, German police later seized four boxes of GM documents that inadvertently had not made it through the shredder. This, combined with the discovery of a letter in which one Lopez aide involved in the shredding operation wrote to another about the necessity to come up with an appropriate cover story to explain their shredding actions, were the first bits of hard evidence used to build GM's case against VW.

The suit was settled out of court in 1997, a year after Lopez left VW to pursue private interests as an automotive consultant. VW was forced to pay GM $100 million in cash and agreed to purchase $1 billion worth of GM auto parts over the next several years. However, because the case never got to trial, the fundamental issue of who owns what information was never fully tested. I do think the message is clear, though.

WHAT IF VW HAD RUN THE OPERATION DIFFERENTLY?

For the purposes of illustration, let's take another look at the GM-VW corporate espionage case from a different perspective. What if a professional CIA-trained case officer had handled that case? If professional clandestine tradecraft techniques had been used by Inaki Lopez's handlers, would Lopez and his coconspirators have been caught? Could they have stolen all of those secrets and gotten away with it? Could VW have avoided the blemish on its reputation and the $1.1 billion settlement, while still benefiting from the information Lopez stole? I submit that it could have. And I'll show you how by reviewing the case step-by-step and injecting some basic operational procedures from Tradecraft 101 into the operation.

First of all, when VW's chairman, Ferdinand Piech, completed his assessment and development of Lopez, he should have immediately moved the operation on to a clandestine level. Instead of broadcasting his desires to make Lopez a part of the VW team, he should have limited knowledge of the operation to a very select few trusted individuals within the company, adopting a "need to know" policy. Then, once he had obtained Lopez's commitment to steal GM's product plans, he should have worked out an arrangement that would have blurred the connection between GM and VW.

In other words, rather than having Lopez suddenly quit GM and move to Germany with six of his closest aides to become a top VW executive with a salary totally off the normal scale, he should have been more discreet. There should have been a grace period between the time Lopez left GM and the time he joined VW. Perhaps Lopez could have concocted a story about having to take a leave of absence or early retirement from GM. Then, maybe a year or so later he would decide to join VW.

Once the time frame and cover story of the defection was established, details involving compensation, communications, and the collection and transportation of the stolen information should have been worked out quietly between Lopez and Piech. The agreement between Piech and Lopez should have been kept totally confidential. Then, in the weeks and months following Piech's recruitment of Lopez, all meetings and communication between them should have been totally clandestine. All talk of Lopez joining VW should have ceased immediately, and all further communications between the two should have been via dead drops, secret writing, encrypted e-mail, and clandestine meetings.

During the hiatus while Lopez was between jobs, he should have been paid through a clandestine, offshore bank account. And, when it came time for him actually to join VW, his acknowledged salary should have been a reasonable one, well within the norm for executive compensation in Germany. The additional compensation could have gone into the offshore account.

Regarding the collection of information, nothing should have been blatantly stolen from GM offices; if nothing was ever reported missing, then nothing could be proved stolen. Lopez and his cohorts should have been given ample time to copy and return whatever corporate documents were needed. Given the volumes of material they took, operational aids like roll-over cameras could have been used to speed up the process and add to the security of the operation. All of this material should have been reduced to film, duplicates made for safekeeping, and copies hand carried to Germany. Debriefings of Lopez and his "warriors" should have occurred in some neutral location; certainly not in the United States or Germany.

If all of these operational principles had been followed, VW would have gotten its information, Lopez and his friends would still be working for VW with healthy clandestine bank accounts in the Cayman Islands, GM would be scratching its corporate head wondering how VW was beating the stuffing out of them competitively, and VW would be $1.1 billion richer.

In short, Piech ran an amateur, arrogant intelligence-gathering operation that failed to protect his sources, and the result was catastrophic for his company and for him personally.

MUSICAL CHAIRS

While the GM-VW case is certainly one of the most egregious examples of luring corporate defectors from one company to another to obtain trade secrets, other examples abound. Jumping from one company to another is especially prevalent in high-tech industries, but not limited to them. Engineers, computer technicians, programmers, and the like move from one company to another with ease. And with each move, information, proprietary and otherwise, moves with them. New employers benefit and old employers lose. It's simply a fact of business.

Some cases have landed in court in recent years: Dow Chemical versus United Polymers, Inc., et al. over a polymer production process sold for more than $4 million; Callaway Golf Company versus Taylor Made Adidas Golf Company over trade secrets regarding the design, manufacture, sale, and marketing of golf balls; Magna International, Inc. versus A. O. Smith Corporation over the theft of a hydroforming process; DEC versus Emulex over proprietary storage technology; Squibb versus Diagnostic Medical Instruments over the theft of designs for cardiac monitoring equipment; Avis versus Hertz over the loss of marketing strategies and operating procedures; GE's medical products division versus Bayer's Agfa group over the theft of electronic medical-imaging technology; Tyson Foods versus ConAgra over the theft of a feed formula; and IBM regularly sues former employees who leave to start new companies for breaches of confidentiality and the theft of IBM's trade secrets. The list is endless, and this is only the tip of the iceberg. Most cases never make it to the litigation stage.

The bottom line is this: the search for secrets crosses the line of legality when a firm pays someone to steal hard-copy confidential information (documents, written notes, tapes, discs, and so forth) from a rival company. The courts do not seem to know exactly where to draw the line between an employee's general knowledge and a company's proprietary information when it's carried within the employee's head. For the most part, they simply won't buy the argument that an employee's thoughts are the property of the employer, and they won't prosecute an offender without hard evidence of a theft. They tend to treat the theft of a file in the same manner as the theft of a car: if the thing stolen is an object that can be seen and touched, the courts will prosecute; if not, they don't want to hear about it.

Employers must also understand that there is a difference between confidentiality agreements and noncompetition agreements. The former strives to restrict the employee from divulging confidential information and usually includes an acknowledgment from the employee concerning what sort of information is of value to the company and should not be disclosed to other parties. The latter strives to prevent an employee from competing with the employer for some specific period of time after termination of employment. Unless confidentiality is also an issue in the noncompete agreement, courts are reluctant to uphold them on the basis that they are in restraint of trade and against public policy.

In any event, employers should always try to protect themselves by having employees sign both confidentiality and noncompete agreements at the time of hiring and again at termination.

TRANSPLANT OPERATIONS AND DOUBLE AGENTS

When the target is particularly elusive and recruiting or inducing the defection of a member of the target group hasn't worked, the next best thing is to dangle an attractive bit of bait in front of the target's nose and hope he snaps it up. The CIA, FBI, and Drug Enforcement Agency (DEA), for example, run these kinds of operations routinely to obtain counterintelligence and intelligence information on enemy targets. An apparently disaffected and vulnerable U.S. military officer is placed in the path of a Russian intelligence officer, or a minor underworld banking figure is recruited to penetrate a major money laundering operation, or an undercover cop is insinuated into the inner family of a major drug cartel. All of these covers and many more have been used in the past to penetrate foreign government, military, and underworld targets by U.S. intelligence and police entities. Books have been written about these kinds of exploits, and Hollywood movies have been made about them.

The idea is to find someone who would be attractive to the target, and then to orchestrate a means to induce the target to accept the "dangle" into the target's group. These kinds of operations require extensive planning and are often very dangerous.

One of the first operations turned over to me as a newly arrived case officer in Saigon during the height of the Vietnam War was a classic and tragic example of a transplant operation.

TUVALOR

Since the agent's real cryptonym is still classified, let's assign him a new one: TUVALOR. (Within the Agency all agents are assigned cryptonyms. These are the names the agents are referred to in all correspondence concerning their operational assignments. The first two letters of a cryptonym is a digraph representing the country they are operating from [in this case the TU represents Vietnam], and the rest of it [VALOR] is a word selected more or less at random from the dictionary. In the CIA, cryptonyms are always typed in upper case.)

TUVALOR was a young major in the South Vietnamese army (ARVN). He and his family were originally from North Vietnam, but like so many other Catholic families, they had fled to the south after the Communist takeover in the north in 1954. The officer was at that time one of the highest-ranking Eurasian—half Vietnamese and half French—officers in the ARVN. Tall and handsome, he was a recognized war hero with three decorations for valor to his credit and had been wounded in combat no fewer than eight times. He was a credit to his French-Vietnamese heritage, to his family, and to the ARVN.

I met TUVALOR for the first time at the Third Field Hospital in Saigon, where he was recovering from his latest injury—shrapnel in his right leg and buttocks. The wounds were received during an abortive attempt by the CIA's Saigon station to smuggle him across the border into Cambodia. TUVALOR's former case officer had attached him to one of the CIA's Provincial Reconnaissance Units (PRU) operating along the Vietnam-Cambodia border, but the team stumbled on a Viet Cong (VC) unit, and in the resultant firefight, TUVALOR was blown off of his feet by a hand grenade.

The purpose of the operation was to have him slip away from the CIA-led PRU team after it was deep within Cambodian territory, and then to dump his uniform and slip into Phnom Penh in mufti. Once in Cambodia's capital, his mission was to walk into the North Vietnamese embassy and ostensibly defect from the ARVN to the Democratic Republic of Vietnam. He would state that in addition to embracing the North Vietnamese cause, he had had enough of killing and never wanted to carry a gun or take another life again. A good plan, a good cover story, but the mission went awry when the team stumbled on a company-sized VC unit, and TUVALOR ended up being hustled back to the Third Field Hospital in Saigon on a stretcher.

The hope was that once the North Vietnamese had established TUVALOR's bona fides to their satisfaction and had benefited from the gold mine of propaganda that would result from the defection of a such a high-profile war hero, they would honor his request to be allowed to spend the rest of the war as a noncombatant pacifist in his native city of Haiphong in North Vietnam. Then, once he was firmly ensconced in the north and all of the publicity surrounding his defection had died down, he would attempt to organize a clandestine intelligence collection net and communicate information out of the country via secret writing to a letter drop in Hong Kong. We would have to wait until TUVALOR was fully recovered before attempting another insertion operation.

I met regularly with TUVALOR in a remote safehouse in the outskirts of Saigon for almost four months while he recovered from his wounds. During this time, TUVALOR was given an intensive review of the clandestine communication methods he was to use to stay in touch with the CIA station in Saigon after he was behind enemy lines.

At the end of the four-month period, TUVALOR was fully proficient in receiving and decoding messages sent to him via one-way voice link (OWVL), and sending messages back to me in Saigon via secret writing (SW). He was also trained in the handling and reading of microdots.

OWVL involved listening to a prearranged regular shortwave broadcast beamed over all of Southeast Asia on a specific frequency. The broadcast consisted of the reading of groups of five numbers. TUVALOR would identify his own agent message by the precise time of the broadcast and hearing his own specific five-number identity group. The identity group would precede the longer, encrypted portion of the message. TUVALOR would copy down the numbers and then later, using a system of "false subtraction" and a miniaturized code book, he would decode and read his message.

Communicating back to Saigon was simpler for TUVALOR. He would first write an innocuous letter to an ostensible relative in Hong Kong (actually an accommodation address rented for him by a support asset in Hong Kong). Then, on the reverse side of the letter he would imprint his secret message using a sort of carbon paper impregnated with invisible ink. When the letter arrived at the accommodation address in Hong Kong, it would be retrieved by the local support asset and delivered to the regional technical support office. There, the SW message would be developed with special chemicals, and the text would be cabled down to the Saigon station for me and my bosses to read.

TUVALOR remained at the Saigon safehouse until his wounds had fully healed, his retraining was complete, and the next phase of the operation was ready for implementation. It was like four months of imprisonment for a man like TUVALOR, but he bore up as well as could be expected throughout the entire ordeal. Then, under our direction, TUVALOR officially disappeared from sight. The ARVN later officially (and reluctantly) listed him as a deserter; even his family and close friends would not be told the real story. As far as they were concerned, TUVALOR had disgraced them and the country he had fought so long and hard for over the years. He had done the unpardonable, and they did not have a "need to know" the true story.

The fact that his family, friends, and former army colleagues now considered him a deserter weighed heavily on his psyche and caused him long periods of depression, but his courage and dedication carried him through. And he knew that things would get worse if the mission were successful and he was indeed accepted as a bona fide defector by North Vietnam. Then his family and friends would regard him as a traitor as well as a deserter. He had placed his full trust and confidence, and indeed his life, in the CIA and his case officers, including yours truly. We repaid that trust by botching the operation and costing TUVALOR his life as well as his reputation.

The new infiltration plan involved using a body smuggler on the station's payroll to insert TUVALOR into Cambodia. The smuggling of ARVN defectors into Cambodia and Thailand was a growth business for the body smugglers of the time. And the practice was extremely profitable for these unscrupulous individuals.

This part of the operation went more or less as planned. Although all of his valuables were stolen en route (by the body smugglers themselves), TUVALOR arrived in Phnom Penh safely with just the clothes on his back. Luckily, we had anticipated this eventuality and had concealed his microdot reader and miniaturized one-time code pads in the soles of his rubber thongs. The Hong Kong accommodation address and location of a downtown Phnom Penh "dead drop" (clandestine hiding place) containing his first supply of money, a few SW carbons, and a microdot message were committed to memory.

After arriving in Phnom Penh, the penniless TUVALOR cleaned himself up as best he could and visited the Phnom Penh library, where he easily located his dead drop under a lower bookshelf in the European history section. He retrieved an envelope containing his supplies and several hundred dollars in Cambodian riels. He then placed one of the thumbtacks that had held the envelope in place in the door jam of the men's room to signal that he had unloaded the drop. He was now fully operational. He left the library and headed for a decent meal, some shopping for clean clothes and toilet articles, and a hotel room where he could get rid of the filth in a hot bath and sleep for twelve uninterrupted hours.

The next morning TUVALOR ate a huge breakfast, purchased a small shortwave radio, and scouted out the North Vietnamese embassy. In the afternoon, he returned to his hotel room to receive and decode his first OWVL broadcast from Saigon station. Following the broadcast, which was aired at precisely 5:17 P.M., he wrote a short cover letter and an SW message stating he had arrived safely, was ready to receive additional OWVL broadcasts, and would be contacting the North Vietnamese embassy the next day.

TUVALOR knocked on the door of the embassy of the Democratic Republic of Vietnam (DRV) just before lunch. He was ushered into a reception room and greeted by a senior North Vietnamese army captain, an intelligence officer. TUVALOR told his story and the North Vietnamese case officer took copious notes. After almost two hours of questioning that sometimes bordered on hostile interrogation, TUVALOR was given an appointment to return to the embassy in two weeks for a follow-up interview. The meeting ended on a high note with the DRV case officer assuring TUVALOR that, if his story checked out, he believed the chances were good that the defection would be accepted and his wish to return to Haiphong would be granted.

The next two weeks were marked by great anticipation both in Saigon and by TUVALOR in Phnom Penh. But when TUVALOR returned to the embassy, the case officer simply said they were not through doing their investigation of his background and scheduled another appointment for a week later. Those of us sitting in Saigon and Langley began to get antsy over this turn of events, but we all agreed that the probable reason for not immediately accepting TUVALOR was because their bureaucracy was just slow in checking him out. We were confident that, in the end, TUVALOR's cover story would check out; we had made sure that his disappearance and previous war record were well publicized in the Saigon press and in ARVN circles. Clearly, we mused, the DRV's sources in Saigon were not as competent and responsive as we had thought them to be.

The next meeting between TUVALOR and the DRV case officer brought more delays. The case officer explained that while they now believed TU-VALOR was who he said he was, they were still unsure about his motivations and his value to the DRV as a noncombatant defector. Then, the case officer suggested that, with the military experience and courage he possessed, TUVALOR would be much more valuable to the DRV as an NVA officer fighting on the front lines against ARVN and U.S. troops. This, of course, was something TUVALOR could not accept (and neither would we, as his CIA backers, authorize), so the DRV vetting process and the dialog dragged on and on. The DRV case officer doled out small amounts of money to TUVALOR to keep him on the string, but weeks ran into months and TUVALOR's and the Saigon station's patience was beginning to run out. It was at this point that an egregious and stupid error was committed by some senior officers monitoring the case at CIA headquarters.

TUVALOR was stopped and questioned by the police one evening after an altercation in a Phnom Penh bar. The police discovered that TUVALOR had no identity papers and threatened to arrest him for illegally entering the country. He bought off the police with a sizable bribe and returned to his hotel room to fire off a desperate SW message to Saigon. He said he was running very low on funds and was afraid the police would continue to keep an eye on him and come back for more baksheesh on a regular basis unless he could get his situation resolved one way or the other as soon as possible. He asked for an immediate cash infusion via dead drop to take care of his immediate needs.

I presented a simple plan to the Saigon chief of station (COS). I suggested we use a reliable station support asset, TUSEED (not the real cryptonym), a French national, to carry money into Phnom Penh and load it into a dead drop for later retrieval by TUVALOR. The COS endorsed the plan, and an immediate cable was sent to CIA headquarters for approval. The following morning, I received the first real disillusioning shock of my career with the Agency.

Headquarters turned down the plan cold. The cable read in part: "WE AT HEADQUARTERS SYMPATHIZE WITH TUVALOR'S SITUA-TION AND THE STATION'S EFFORTS TO ALLEVIATE IT. HOW-

EVER, FROM OUR OPTIC IT APPEARS THAT TUVALOR'S ARREST CAN ONLY SERVE TO ENHANCE HIS COVER IN CAMBODIA. WE THEREFORE DO NOT RPT NOT AUTHORIZE THE USE OF TUSEED, OR ANY OTHER STATION SUPPORT ASSET, TO SERVICE TUVALOR VIA DEAD DROP IN PHNOM PENH."

The COS and I were furious. But despite several heated back-channel cable exchanges between the COS and headquarters, the order stood. I informed TUVALOR, who by this time had been shaken down by the police once again and was now totally out of cash, of headquarters' decision via an OWVL broadcast. I also instructed TUVALOR to return to the DRV embassy and redouble his pleas to his North Vietnamese case officer to accept his defection and give him money and protection. Headquarters was betting everything on the chance that the North Vietnamese would accelerate their vetting process and accept TUVALOR rapidly.

About three weeks later, we received a letter via the Hong Kong accommodation address. The SW message on the reverse side of the letter will forever be burned into my memory. It read: "WHY DO YOU NOT SEND ME MONEYx I CAN STAND IT NO LONGERx VERY BAD SCENE HEREx NV EMBASSY TAKING TOO MUCH TIME TO MAKE UP MIND BUT I WILL COMPLETE MY MISSIONx I WILL CACHE RADIO AND OT PADS IN A SAFE PLACE AND JOIN VC TO GO NORTHx I STILL HAVE MICRODOT READER AND HONGKONG ADDRESSx WILL WRITE YOU LETTER WHEN I ARRIVE IN HAIPHONGx END END END END."

TUVALOR had cached his commo equipment and had found another way to get to North Vietnam and fulfill his mission. He had somehow joined up with a Viet Cong unit heading north up the Ho Chi Minh trail. Resourcefulness was a prime virtue in an agent, and TUVALOR was a superb agent.

The agent had no way of knowing that swarms of giant B-52s would soon be running saturation bombing missions on the Ho Chi Minh trail all along the border between Vietnam and Cambodia. We never heard from TUVALOR again.

A year later he was officially declared "presumed dead," and a courier delivered an unmarked envelope containing $10,000 in cash to his family in Saigon.

TUVALOR's personnel file was closed and retired to archives. The Agency forgot about TUVALOR, and to this day his family and friends still think he was a deserter.

THE HIRING OF SOURCES

So when Hitech, Inc., wants to acquire information on Highertech, Inc., and they can't induce the defection (hire) of one of Highertech's engineers, the next best thing would be to select a suitable Hitech employee and dangle him or her in front of Highertech's Human Resources department. If the double-agent is accepted and hired by Highertech, Hitech will benefit in two ways: it will learn what information Highertech has and wishes to acquire on Hitech (counterintelligence information), and it will gain positive intelligence on Highertech's plans, intentions, processes, and any other confidential information within the reach of the planted agent. An additional advantage is that the information provided by the source is the same as any penetration agent: not just historical as in the case of a defector, but also up-to-date information along with projections for the future.

Let me say a word or two about the qualities of a double agent. The individual selected must be thoroughly vetted and totally loyal. Working within the enemy camp is extremely stressful and sometimes quite dangerous, so careful agent handling is a must. Meetings between the agent and case officer must be clandestine, and any information obtained must be closely guarded (the "need to know" principle should be strictly enforced), and no action on any information directly obtained from the source that could in any way jeopardize the agent can ever be taken.

These are limiting factors on the effectiveness of the double agent. But since the characteristics that make a good double agent are the same characteristics that can lead to his being spotted (for example, coming from a trusted position within the inner circle of a competing company—possibly even a family member of that company), it is important that they be strictly adhered to.

These kinds of esoteric operations clearly are beyond the competence of most companies, but foreign intelligence services use them all the time. They have the training, experience, and resources at their disposal to make them work. So beware the Chinese exchange technician, Russian graduate student, or any other foreign technician or engineer whose loyalties may be primarily with his or her home country.

We'll be discussing this subject in greater depth in the chapter on counterintelligence.

5

AUDIO OPERATIONS

The first thing I must say to you regarding audio operations (bugging, telephone taps) is don't even consider doing one; the second thing is to warn you not to allow yourself to become a victim of one.

Although audio operations are a mainstay of the CIA's clandestine services and of the FBI, they are illegal in the United States (and in most other countries) without a court order, signed by a judge, authorizing them in very specific instances. That is not to say, however, that unscrupulous private investigators and individuals engaged in corporate and economic espionage will hesitate to break the law if the expected rewards are great enough—if the risks justify the possible gains. So, at the risk of making you paranoid, I'm going to describe the various types of audio operations and show you how they are planned and executed by professionals. By knowing what they are and how they are implemented, you will be better able to defend yourself against attack.

THE TROJAN HORSE
Beware of Greeks bearing gifts! One of the most popular forms of audio operation is the Trojan horse. Simply put, it is a method of planting a listening device concealed in a gift given to the target by someone working for the

target's adversary. The hope is that, when the bugged gift arrives, it is of such a nature that it will be placed in an area where the target holds his most private conversations; the board room or on his office desk, for example. The type of gift will therefore determine the location within the target office that it will most likely be placed. Once the gift is given, the gift giver has no control over where it will end up.

One of the most unique and innovative Trojan horse operations I was ever involved in was run against a high-priority Communist embassy target a few years ago. During a diplomatic dinner party at the home of one of my access agents, one of the guests, who happened to be the ambassador of the target country, admired a sculpture prominently displayed in the agent's living room.

The half-life-size bronze statue depicted an old farmer with his head thrown back and his smiling face looking toward the sun. The ambassador read great meaning into the sculpture—bleak poverty with a promise of a new dawning. He felt the symbolism represented his country's struggling attempts to move out of the old ways of the past and into the bright new future of the modern world.

When the agent reported this information, an idea began to germinate in the heads of the station case officers working on the target. Why not present the ambassador with a gift of the sculpture? Surely he would display it in a conspicuous, honored place within the embassy; perhaps in the conference room where embassy meetings took place, or maybe in the main salon where visitors were met and interviewed. The agent was asked to bring the statue to the safehouse at his next agent meeting so that it could be examined by one of the Agency's audio technicians.

When the tech saw the statue, he immediately noted that although it was certainly large enough, there was no way to install a microphone and transmitter, along with a sufficient supply of batteries and a remote switch to ensure enough life to make the operation worthwhile, without noticeably marring the statue.

Often the problem with stand-alone concealments for audio devices was that, since they had to draw their power from batteries, and batteries only last so long, the more you put into a device the bigger and heavier it becomes. Miniaturization has come a long way for all component parts except batteries. Installing a switch that enables the transmitter to be turned on and off from a remote location can extend the battery life considerably by shortening the time the transmitter is drawing power from the batteries in the on position.

In most cases, we are looking for years of transmitter life rather than a few weeks or months. A three-foot-high bronze statue is certainly an ideal concealment in which to load a bunch of batteries and equipment, but the trick in this case was how to get all of the stuff in there without leaving noticeable scars on the outside of the statue.

So we had to give it more thought. Cables flew back and forth between the station and CIA headquarters and the regional tech base. Finally, we were presented with a viable alternative by the audio technicians: sculpt an identical copy of the original statue and install the audio equipment into it before the final casting is made. In other words, we wouldn't present the ambassador with the original sculpture; we would give him a bugged copy of the original.

Luckily, one of the audio techs was a very good sculptor, so he was selected to create a copy of the original statue. While he was busy copying the statue, other techs assembled and tested the microphone, transmitter, switch, and a year's supply of batteries for later installation in the old man's head.

The result was really quite amazing. The sculpture rendered by the tech sculptor was a remarkable copy. Even the weight of the finished product was not noticeably different from the original. And an unexpected plus occurred when the device was fully assembled and enclosed in the statue. The microphone was positioned behind the upturned mouth of the old man, and the resultant audio quality, enhanced by the hollow head, was incredibly rich and deep and clear.

Now all we had to do was to have the agent present the statue to his friend, the ambassador, and then monitor the results. We waited for an auspicious occasion—the Communist country's National Day—to present the gift. It was accomplished during an evening reception at the embassy.

Our surveillance team watched the agent arrive at the embassy compound, remove the wrapped statue from the trunk of his car, and carry it into the chancery building. The device was switched on remotely as the agent walked through the front door, and the entire presentation was monitored live by the surveillance team. A permanent listening post had been set up in an apartment a block away, and it was there that the actual recording of the audio took place.

The ambassador was delighted with the gift. He set it up on one of the serving tables for all to admire, and we recorded diplomatic chit chat–type conversations in its vicinity throughout the evening. Then, when the last guest had departed, the room was closed and the ambassador and his staff retired for the night. The device was then switched off remotely from the listening post.

It was turned on again early the following morning and people could be heard bustling about in the morning hours, drinking tea and preparing for the day ahead. Then the ambassador entered the room with his secretary and they discussed his schedule for the day. That discussion was followed by a regular morning staff meeting. People could be heard gathering in the room and snippets of conversation among staff members were recorded.

The staff meeting began promptly at 9:00 A.M., and the audio device performed beautifully, recording every word spoken with outstanding audio quality. The transcripts provided the information for the first two intelligence reports generated by the operation.

At the end of the briefing, however, the ambassador was heard ordering one of the embassy workmen to place the sculpture at the top of the stairs leading to the second floor of the chancery "so that everyone in the embassy could admire it." Unfortunately for us, this placed the audio device in what was essentially a hallway within the embassy, not a very good place to record conversations among the staff and visitors.

In short, the operation was a resounding success, but the patient died. After a few weeks of futile monitoring of footsteps on the stairs and bits and pieces of conversation as people walked past the old man, the operation was terminated. The device was turned off for good, and the listening post was vacated and shut down.

That is precisely the problem with Trojan horse audio operations, the gift giver usually has no control over where the gift will be placed. Another major drawback to these kinds of operations is that everyone knows exactly where the gift came from. So, if the device is ever discovered by the target, the accusing finger is immediately pointed directly at the person who gave the gift in the first place. And that could mean death to an agent.

THE QUICK PLANT

Another way to introduce an audio device into a target is the quick plant. Although the problem with this type of operation is that it requires direct access to the target area—someone actually has to be there to physically slap the audio device under a conference table or whatever—it has certain definite advantages over the Trojan horse. Most of all, there usually is no direct link between the agent who plants the device and the device itself. (I'll explain what I mean by "usually" a little later on.) And this is a huge advantage.

There are also varying degrees of quick plants, but all require some sort of basic casing of the target before a device can be planted. For example, if the device is to be placed under a conference table, it would be best to know in advance whether the table is made of dark or light wood so that the device will not be immediately apparent to anyone who makes a casual inspection of the underside of the table, something that should be a routine security precaution for anyone guarding proprietary information. The possibility of at least a visual inspection should be considered in advance of any such operation.

As with the Trojan horse, concealment plays a major role in the success of quick plant operations. In the case of a conference table, for example, it would be far better to conceal the audio device in a block of wood that perfectly matches one of the triangular corner braces of the table than to use a square block of wood that resembles nothing else under the table. The latter wouldn't pass even a casual inspection by a security officer, whereas the former might go unnoticed for years.

This is why I said earlier that there "usually" isn't a direct link between the agent who installs a quick plant device and the target. If the concealment is bad and the device is recognized soon after the installation, or worse, if the agent is caught in the act of installing the device, clearly the linkage will be a huge problem for the agent.

Concealments for quick plant devices can be tailored or generic. Examples of tailored concealments include the triangular corner brace discussed above that can be installed under conference, coffee, or other kinds of tables, or a book that can be slipped in among other similar books on a bookshelf. You are only limited by your imagination in cases such as these.

Generic concealments that have been used successfully in the past include a ruler or screwdriver that can be casually slipped between the cushions of a couch, or my favorite, the multiple wall plug AC adapter. You know, that common three-pronged electrical thing you plug into an electrical outlet receptacle to convert it into one that will handle three or more appliances.

The beauty of this concealment is that it is very common—multiple adapters are found in electrical outlets all over the world—and when one is "inadvertently" left behind in a target's outlet, it won't attract any attention whatsoever (as long as it matches the adapters commonly used in a particular country). An added plus is that it also does not require batteries; electricity to run the device is drawn directly from the outlet, so its lifespan is unlimited.

There are drawbacks to this multiple plug adapter audio device as well, however, as the following story will illustrate.

The CIA had been working to penetrate a high-priority Asian country's embassy for many years without success. Then, following a major political incident involving that country and the United States, several friendly (to the Asian country) news agencies were asked by the country's spokeswoman to come to the embassy for some substantive television interviews to explain their position. This would require film crews to support the reporters for each of the news agencies.

Fortunately for us, one of our longtime access agents was a technician for one of the film crews—he would be in charge of setting up the lights and cameras to record the interviews. And of course, this would involve plugging things into wall outlets where multiple plug adapters would be required.

On the day of the interview, a surveillance van was parked nearby to monitor and record the installation of the audio device. The news crew arrived on schedule and entered the embassy to set up for the interview. As soon as our agent plugged the audio device into the wall, we got good, clear audio from the room. The interview was recorded without a hitch, and when the crew packed up its equipment, our agent left the device plugged into the wall socket. The private conversations that took place among the embassy staff members after the film crew had left resulted in an excellent intelligence report on the country's planned diplomatic and media plans.

The audio device remained plugged into the socket in the reception room of the embassy for several more weeks, where it monitored a number of interesting conversations between staff members and visitors. The result was a steady stream of reports of great intelligence and operational value. Then suddenly the device went dead.

On the day of its demise, the cleaning lady could be heard rummaging around the room, dusting and polishing and putting the room into order. Then she plugged her vacuum cleaner into the adapter device and proceeded to vacuum the floor. When she was through with her vacuuming she unplugged the vacuum, leaving the audio device still attached to the vacuum cord. Robbed of its power source, the device stopped transmitting.

We continued to check for audio over the next several months, but the only thing we ever heard was the sound of vacuuming when the cleaning lady plugged her vacuum into the wall. When she was through, however, the vacuum (and our device) went back into the cleaning closet. Although we all prayed that she might eventually leave the device behind, plugged into a socket in a good location, it never happened, and the operation was eventually reluctantly terminated.

That's the biggest problem with these kinds of quick plant audio devices; once the device is planted, control over its placement is lost forever.

DRILLING OPERATIONS

One of the most successful audio operations in CIA history occurred in Europe several years ago. The intelligence produced by the operation was so voluminous and of such high quality that it made heroes of all those case officers and technicians involved in its conception and implementation. On the operational side, that included me as the principal case officer for the operation, up through the ranks to my branch chief, the station chief, the division chief back at CIA headquarters, and the Agency's deputy director of operations—the DDO. It was also instrumental in promoting the diplomatic careers of several other high-ranking State Department and National Security Council officials who vicariously basked in the importance of the information the operation provided at a critical time in history.

The target building was, as you might guess, again a very high-priority Asian embassy. From the day of my arrival to the day of my departure almost four years later, the penetration of that embassy was my main operational task and obsession.

My early days at the station were spent in the office poring over files that contained detailed casings of the lower floor (none of our agents had ever been permitted to venture above the first floor), which consisted of two salons—one large and one small—a small reception area, and a restroom. We had also acquired descriptions of the furniture, the paintings on the walls, the lamps, knickknacks, and other smaller accoutrements in the rooms. Several Trojan horse and quick plant operations had been suggested but rejected for one reason or another. One of these involved the possible switching of a Courvoisier Cannon that sat prominently on one of the coffee tables, but it was rejected because of the difficulty of making the exchange (the cannon frame was too bulky to fit into something, like a briefcase, to carry into the building) and the lack of sufficient space in the frame to conceal the audio equipment and batteries.

So, it wasn't long before I started focusing on a building that appeared to share a common wall with the embassy; an apartment house that was built smack up against the rear of our target building. The building consisted of four stories, with two small apartments on the first floor and one larger apartment on each of the other higher floors. All of the apartments shared parts of the common wall with the embassy, so any one of them would offer access to somewhere in the embassy by drilling through the common wall.

I became obsessed with that building, walking past it several times a day, sitting in a café across the street for hours at a time, just staring at it and watching people come and go and learning everything I could about its occupants.

Our first break came when I noticed that the window of the ground floor apartment on the street side was shuttered for three days in a row. This was unusual, because I had never seen it remain shuttered for more than a day before. This prompted me to peek through a crack in the shutters. When I did, I discovered that the apartment was totally empty. The occupants had apparently moved out, and this could only mean that the apartment was now for rent. I knew that if we could rent that apartment, we could drill through the back wall directly into the embassy's small salon. I was excited and needed to move fast.

Since there were no "for rent" signs on the building, I decided to send one of my support assets, a cherubic fellow we called "Jo-Jo," to inquire among the occupants of the building regarding the vacant apartment. He learned that the couple who lived there had indeed left for good, and that the apartment rental was being handled by a local real estate agent. Jo-Jo immediately hotfooted it over to the real estate office to inquire about renting the apartment. He was, unfortunately, told that it had already been rented by friends of the couple who had been living there, and that they were expected to sign a contract within the next couple of days.

When Jo-Jo reported this news to me a few hours later in a nearby café, I was initially just disappointed. But the longer I thought about it, the more inclined I was not to take "no" for an answer. After all, the real estate agent had said the contract had not yet been signed. I seized upon that bit of information and decided to act upon it immediately. I told my agent to wait for me in the café while I hurried back to my office to grab the equivalent of about $2,000 in crisp new bills from my operational revolving fund. I put the stack of bills in a plain white envelope, sealed it, and stuffed it in my jacket pocket. Then I returned to the café and pushed the bulging package of notes across the table to Jo-Jo.

I instructed him to return immediately to the real estate agent and tell him that he needed that exact apartment because it suited his needs perfectly; virtually no other apartment would do for him. I told him to beg, scream, cry, do whatever it would take, but not to return without that apartment. We worked out a story whereby Jo-Jo would say that his wife needed a ground floor apartment because she was confined to a wheelchair, and she needed to be in that particular neighborhood because it was her childhood neighborhood and he was bringing her back there to die. If that wouldn't pull at his heartstrings, we thought, nothing would.

I sat in that café, drinking one espresso after another, until Jo-Jo returned about an hour and a half later. I could tell by his face that he didn't get the apartment.

Jo-Jo nervously related what took place during his meeting with the real estate agent. He said he went through his act, crying and begging, but the agent stoically stuck to his position that he had given his word to the couple and could not back down. Then Jo-Jo pulled the envelope from his pocket, slid it across the desk to the real estate agent, and made a last plea for him to use the money in the envelope to help find the couple another apartment, but to give him this one; it was that important to him. The real estate agent slowly picked up the envelope, hefted it as if to divine the amount of money within, turned, tossed it into a cabinet safe behind his desk, and calmly told Jo-Jo, "I'll see what I can do."

Not the least of my concerns over receiving this news was that I had not obtained authorization from any of my superiors, not my branch chief nor the station chief, for an expenditure this large. So, without even a receipt to show where the money went, if we weren't successful in getting the apartment, I was going to be out of pocket $2,000. And this was something I could ill afford in those days.

Late the following afternoon Jo-Jo returned to the real estate office to receive the news concerning the apartment rental. As soon as he left the real estate office, he signaled for a meeting with me. I got to the café a few minutes before him and watched as he approached. I could see the excitement in his eyes and when he sat down he took my hand in both of his and exclaimed, "I've got it!" We were in business.

Now we were home free, or so it seemed. We had an apartment in the building that not only could provide us with audio access to an important room in the embassy, the small salon, but would also give us a listening post from which we could monitor and record all of the conversations from the target. Furthermore, as an added plus, it could serve as a base of operations for obtaining temporary access to additional apartments in the building from which we could penetrate into additional rooms in the embassy. With all of this good fortune, disaster struck on our first drilling attempt.

By the time the audio techs arrived to do the actual drilling and installation of the microphone and wire, Jo-Jo had moved into the little apartment (without his fictitious wheelchair-bound wife) and had set up housekeeping as a normal resident of the neighborhood. He walked his little dog around the neighborhood, meeting the shopkeepers and neighbors, and generally became part of the local scene.

On the day of the drilling operation, we smuggled the two disguised audio techs into the apartment during the morning rush hour, and they immediately went about unloading their tools and audio gear from the three large hard-backed Samsonite suitcases they had carried in with them. They then put the drill to the kitchen wall above the sink and started to push through the reinforced concrete toward the small salon on the other side.

They had estimated that the total thickness of the two contiguous walls was about thirty to thirty-two inches, so they had a lot of drilling to do before coming close to the other side, where the operation would become really delicate. They decided to use a one-and-a-half-inch core drill for the first eighteen inches. This would put them well into the target wall before they would switch to a smaller, quieter three-eighths-inch drill bit for the remainder of the drilling.

They planned to use the three-eighths-inch drill bit until they were about three inches from the end. At that point they would begin using a probe device called a "back-scatter gauge" to measure the exact distance from the end of the drill hole to the other (target) side of the wall. Then, when the back-scatter gauge indicated they were within a half to three-eighths of an inch from the end, they would put aside the three-eighths-inch drill and use a tiny pin-sized drill called a "pin vise" for the remainder of the drilling into the room on the other side. All that was required for the microphone to work properly was this pin-sized tunnel of air; the tiny pinhole would not be visible from the other side, and the sausage-shaped three-eighths-inch microphone would fit snuggly in the shaft up against the pinhole. This is what was supposed to happen.

What actually happened was a total screwup. The audio tech who was doing the drilling had been traveling extensively in Africa doing other audio installations and was exhausted and jet-lagged when he reached our location. I have no idea what was going through his mind when he started on this job, but his mind was clearly not on his work. He started with the one-and-a-half-inch core drill bit and pushed it through the first eighteen inches of concrete without a problem. The construction was old and the concrete was sandy, so the work went swiftly. He then switched to the three-eighths-inch bit and, apparently without thinking, and without ever checking his depth with the back-scatter gauge, pushed it straight through the remainder of the wall and out through the other side into the embassy's small salon.

He stood ashen-faced and trembling on the ladder, all six-feet-two and 200 pounds of him, with his left hand plastered over the hole and his other holding the long drill at his side, loudly whispering at the rest of us standing behind him, "I broke through! I broke through the fucking wall!" The other tech handed him a large sponge to stick in the hole, and I told him to get down from the ladder before he fell off of it. When he stepped down, I mounted the ladder, asked for the lights to be turned off in the room, removed the sponge, and peered through the channel into the room on the other side. Thank God no one was there at the time. I remember thinking, "Yep, it looks exactly like the casings said it would look like."

We then regrouped and planned our next moves. We had no idea what the wall now looked like from the other side, or whether the tech had had his finger on the water trigger of the drill when he broke through, thereby squirting a long, wet streak of dirty water across the room. All we knew for sure was that there was now a three-eighths-inch hole in the middle of the target's wall, and there was no way to examine it or to restore it to its original condition from our side.

We had to get out of there fast, but first we had to do whatever we could to limit the damage. The first step was to try to plug the hole as best we could from our side. The tech removed the end piece of concrete from the core drill and we noted that it contained a layer of painted plaster on one end. He took some measurements of the depth of the hole and prepared the core with epoxy cement to be reinserted into the hole and glued back into place. When he thought he had his measurements right, he pushed the core back into the hole until he reached the spot where he estimated it was flush with the other side, and left it there for the glue to harden. At this point, we had no idea how close to the end he had gotten, or even whether the core was now sticking out of the hole on the other side.

The two techs then busied themselves filling and plastering the hole from the kitchen side, cleaning up, and packing up their gear. Jo-Jo was also busy packing. I had instructed him to leave the city immediately and to join his family in the south where they were vacationing. I told him to stay there until I could contact him. If the operation was discovered by the target occupants, and we assumed it would be at this point, he was instructed to deny any knowledge of it. He would just say that he was vacationing with his family at a coastal resort in the south and someone must have broken into his apartment without his knowledge or consent. Given the nature of the operation, this story was certainly plausible.

So with the apartment vacated and cleaned up and the two audio techs on their way back to the regional tech base and Jo-Jo on his way to the coast, I headed back to the station to give the bad news to my station chief. It was not a pleasant task.

Then we all hunkered down with bated breath to await the discovery and the (you know what) to hit the fan. But days passed and nothing happened. Still more days passed and still nothing happened. When a full two weeks had passed, we decided to send one of our access agents to the embassy to try to take a look at the damaged wall from the inside. He arranged an appointment with one of the embassy officials and was met in the small salon, where he casually noted every nick and blemish on the back wall of the room. Although he wasn't told why we had levied this odd requirement on him, it didn't take him long to figure it out.

When he met with his station case officer a few hours after the interview the first words out of his mouth were: "What the hell did you guys do?" He then went on to describe the damage to the wall in the exact place we had told him it probably was located. He said there was a perfectly round three-eighths-inch indentation in the center of the wall at about sitting eye level. It was about three feet away from him as he sat talking to the embassy official. He said the indentation was about an eighth of an inch deep, and "it looked like someone had hit the wall with the handle end of a broom and dented the plaster."

Despite his egregious error in breaking through the wall in the first place, the audio tech had done a superb job of repairing the damage from the inside out. Now at least we knew what we were dealing with.

We waited a few more weeks and, with everything still quiet, we decided to go back in and do it right this time. I traveled down to the coast to meet and brief the agent, and a new pair of well-rested audio techs prepared to come to town for round two.

This time the operation was accomplished without a hitch. We drilled a new hole a few feet to the left of the old one and used the pin vise to create an air passage into the room. The audio quality was outstanding.

The only difference between the planning of this operation and the first one was that originally we had intended to run a wire from the microphone in the wall directly to a tape recorder in the kitchen of the access apartment. This was called a "microphone and wire" operation. It is the simplest and most reliable of all of these kinds of audio operations, but it has one major drawback: the wire connected to the microphone in the wall of the target leads directly to the listening post. So if the target occupants discover the pinhole and microphone, all they have to do is follow the wire to find the culprits.

So, to provide our agent with a degree of "plausible denial" in case the operation were eventually discovered, we decided to hook the microphone to a switched transmitter; something we could turn on and off remotely and monitor from anywhere within a 500-yard radius. This way we could move the listening post away from the agent's apartment, and he could still play the dupe if he were ever questioned about the operation.

The switched transmitter was concealed in the wall behind the microphone and hooked up to an AC current line so it would never run out of power. An LP (listening post) was acquired in another building in the neighborhood, and monitoring began.

The take from this operation exceeded all of our expectations. The small salon was used for most of the target's meetings and interviews with foreigners as well as for regular staff briefings and discussions. A particularly fruitful staff gathering, usually including briefings by official visitors from the home country, took place every Thursday evening after dinner. A steady stream of intelligence reports was generated, creating a growing need for more transcribers and reports officers, and operational information including biographic data and personality assessments on staff and visiting officials was filling files back at CIA headquarters. Kudos abounded for this once-damned operation.

But the fear was still there that one day one of the occupants would notice the blemish on the wall and call the security folks who would discover our penetration. That was until one day about six months after the breakthrough occurred when something totally unexpected happened; something that turned out to be manna from heaven.

One morning, as our LP keeper was monitoring from his nearby apartment, several workmen were heard entering the room amid the clattering of tools and buckets. They turned out to be painters. As they were inspecting the walls for sanding and spackling one of them could be heard standing directly in front of our three-eighths-of-an-inch breakthrough scar. He shouted to one of the others, "Come here. Look at this. What is this?" One of the other painters, probably the boss, came over and examined the indentation and replied, "It's a hole." The other said, "Well what do you want to do about it?" The boss replied, "Fix it."

And that's what they did. They spackled the hole and painted the room, covering forever the evidence of our earlier disaster.

But the story of this operation doesn't end there. We went on to use Jo-Jo as an access agent to develop relationships with the other residents of the apartment building, and his ground floor apartment as a staging area for several more audio penetrations of the embassy.

The first of these was an audio penetration of the large salon, located at the other end of the embassy on the same floor as the small salon. It was adjacent to another small apartment in the rear of the building, occupied by an elderly couple.

Jo-Jo befriended them and quickly learned that they would be vacationing for the entire month of August (like most other Europeans) on the sunny Mediterranean coast. Since it was already mid-July, only two weeks from their vacation, we had to move fast. We already knew that the elderly couple's apartment shared a common wall with the embassy's large salon, but we had to figure a way to gain access to the apartment while the couple was out of town on vacation. Jo-Jo tried offering to keep an eye on the place while they were away, but they replied that it wasn't necessary—they said they would just lock the door and leave.

An examination of the door lock showed it to be a high security, round-key type that was extremely difficult to pick, so we decided to try to get a copy of the key before the couple left. This was accomplished a few days later while Jo-Jo and the couple were enjoying an aperitif in the couple's apartment. While the woman was busying herself in the kitchen and the man was visiting the toilet, and the keys were sitting on a small table near the door, Jo-Jo used his key impression kit to copy the key.

The key impression kit is a simple little pocket-sized, aluminum, hinged waffle iron–type device filled with modeling clay. The device is opened, the key pressed into the bed of clay on one side, then closed and pressed firmly shut to gain an impression of the other side. When the device is opened and the key is gently removed, a full impression of the key remains imbedded in the clay. A duplicate key can then easily be made from the impression.

We were now prepared to enter the apartment when the couple was vacationing on the Mediterranean coast and to drill into the large salon of the embassy.

The operation was completed in one day. The techs were infiltrated in the morning, and Jo-Jo and I kept an eye on the apartment building door and did whatever else we could to make sure the techs had a secure operating environment within which to work.

Because there appeared to be a lot of activity within the room, as an added precaution we decided not to do the final drilling and pin vising until we were sure no one was in the large salon. We were within an inch or two of the end by midafternoon, so we sent Jo-Jo out to walk his dog around the building to see if any lights were on in the room. He reported that there were, so we waited, and waited, sending Jo-Jo out to check every hour or so. Finally, at around 9:00 P.M., the lights went out.

The techs completed the drilling and gently used the pin vise to create an air passage into the room. We then tested the audio by pushing the little sausage-shaped microphone down the three-eighths-inch tunnel and seeding it tight up against the airhole. Earphones were then hooked to the wire, and the tech slipped them on to listen. As soon as he put them on, he abruptly ripped them off of his head and exclaimed, "Holy shit, there's a war going on in there!"

We had apparently waited until the entire staff of the embassy was assembled in the room to watch a war movie. The tech had heard the sounds of explosions and the whistling of ricocheting bullets.

While the take from this operation did not equal that of the small salon, it was still very good. Larger staff briefings were held in the room as well as cocktail parties and bull sessions among the staff, and some interviews with foreigners were conducted there when the small salon was being used. Our nearby LP keeper was now monitoring and recording two separate audio operations, putting a further strain on our limited transcription, translation, and reporting resources. We requested that more people be assigned to the project, and headquarters hastily complied. This surprised those of us used to bureaucratic foot-dragging until we learned that the operation was turning into a Godsend for those once intelligence-starved analysts working on the target country.

Our next attempt held great promise. It was an effort to penetrate the ambassador's office, and it came after an extensive evaluation of light patterns in the embassy. Briefly, what we did was to have Jo-Jo watch the windows in the building and note the times lights went on and off. Lights that were on during the day and turned off at night usually meant they were offices, and lights that were off during the day and turned on only at night were usually living quarters.

Our attention was drawn to an office on the top floor, rear of the embassy, which backed up on our contiguous apartment building. The lights in this office were on all day and well into the evening hours when all of the other offices were vacated for the day. Several things militated for an attack on this room. First, it could be accessible to us because it shared a common wall with our building; second, it was on the top floor of the embassy, where most ambassador's offices would be located; third, the ambassador had a reputation of being a workaholic, often working late into the night. For all of these reasons, it was certainly worth a shot.

Because of the juxtaposition of the two buildings, the apartment building being about three to four feet higher at the street level because of the slope of the road, we figured that the top (third) floor of the apartment building would still share the bottom half of the wall of the fourth floor of the embassy building. In other words, if we drilled near the ceiling of the access apartment we would come out just above the baseboard of the embassy room.

The occupants of the third-floor apartment were an old woman and her spinster daughter, a plain woman in her mid-forties. Jo-Jo had met them on several occasions and was able to elicit a considerable amount of personal information from them. For example, we knew where the daughter worked during the day, and that the old lady rarely left the apartment except for short periods to shop in the neighborhood. They did not own a car and remained in the city during the hot summer holidays. We also learned that the daughter had very little social life beyond her immediate family. We decided to use this last point to develop closer access to the pair for the purpose of gaining access to the apartment for long enough to do our drilling thing.

We chose a support agent named Richard for the job. Richard was a handsome, polished, fiftyish male escort. He could charm the socks off women of all ages and was socially well connected. The poor spinster wouldn't stand a chance. In fact, after their first (engineered, of course) chance encounter, it took Richard less than a week to elicit an invitation to the spinster's apartment to meet her mother. During this meeting, he took professional photos of the two women, with the common wall in their living room as a backdrop behind them. This requirement was necessary because we would need to restore the wall to its original condition after we finished messing it up with our drilling job. We needed to know in advance the color, condition, wallpaper, trim color, material, and so forth in order to make our plans for a perfect restoration job.

Richard was also tasked to obtain a copy of the key to the apartment. We had already determined that the lock was not a difficult one to pick—it was a normal flat-key pin and tumbler lock—but having a key in our possession just made the job of entering the apartment that much quicker and easier. Picking locks is not as easy as it is portrayed in the movies. An experienced locksmith can spend minutes or hours working on the same lock. It's very much a matter of feel and luck when it comes to how long it takes, and we wanted to avoid having a tech on his knees in front of the door for an extended period of time when we were ready to go.

So Richard's next order of business was to obtain a copy of the front door key. This was accomplished during a dinner at a popular local restaurant during their first "date." Richard had selected this particular restaurant because of the many distractions there; it was a huge, bustling place where people went to see and be seen. It was also just around the corner from a department store that had a key-duplicating machine.

During the meal Richard slipped the spinster's keys out of her bag and pocketed them. A little later he excused himself to make a phone call and slipped out of the restaurant. He then hurried directly to the key-duplicating machine in the department store and had a copy made, returning to the spinster's side no more than ten minutes later. The woman's keys went back into her bag and the duplicate remained in Richard's pocket. Swift and easy access in and out of the apartment was now assured. Now Richard concentrated on the next phase of the operation.

After several more dates over the next few weeks Richard suggested that the woman and her mother join him for a relaxing weekend in the countryside. He told them about his charming little cottage on the southern coast and suggested they drive out there for a few days. The offer was enthusiastically accepted and plans were made. Meanwhile, the techs and I were making our own plans to coincide with Richard's.

A couple weeks later, early on a Saturday morning, Richard picked up the women at their apartment and headed out of town for the weekend. Our surveillance watched them depart and stayed with them until they were on the turnpike heading west out of town. The techs and I then entered the apartment and began drilling into what we thought was the ambassador's office.

The operation, including a difficult restoration that involved delicately peeling back a portion of the old wallpaper and regluing it perfectly back in place, went without a hitch. The audio quality was excellent, and our LP keeper now had three separate installations to monitor and record.

The bad news was that the room turned out to be the embassy administrative office, and not the ambassador's office, so the intelligence generated was minimal compared to that of the two salons and our expectations. But the good news was that we gained an important operational lead from one of the early conversations recorded in the room. We heard the admin officers talking about the high-level meetings that were held in the "secret room" while one of the visiting dignitaries was there. They described the room as being "across the hall," which would put it at the other end of the building adjacent to one of the bedrooms in the spinster's apartment. We decided to go back.

The original blueprints of what was now the embassy building showed two rooms on the upper floor in the rear of the building on the other side of the stairs from the admin office. The secret room had to be one of these rooms, but since we didn't know which one, we decided to bug both of them.

Richard had kept in touch with the spinster during the intervening weeks, so we instructed him to rekindle the relationship and to make a repeat trip to the southern coast with the ladies. We would need another undisturbed weekend to do the two installations. So Richard turned on the charm and we ended up back in the apartment poking holes in the common wall.

The first installation was into the middle room of the embassy. We got good audio quality and heard the sounds of conversations and typewriters from the room. We then installed our audio equipment in the wall, restored everything to its original condition, and moved on to the end room. Since the middle room was clearly an office, this had to be the secret room.

The drilling again went without a hitch, but when we pin vised through the last half inch into the room, our audio was muffled. We listened for almost two hours but only heard the muffled sounds of street noise and ambient noises from within the building. We were puzzled. The fact that there may not have been anyone in the room to listen to at the time did not negate the problem of the generally poor audio. The ambient noise was muffled, and so even if we were able to monitor a conversation from within the room, that conversation would probably be muffled as well.

We tried another microphone with the same result, and then used the pin vise to widen the airhole, but this didn't work either. The techs then suggested that we might not actually be in the room itself, but only in a cavity in the wall close to the other side. They suggested drilling a bit farther with the three-eighths-inch drill, essentially drilling through the cavity back through to the solid wall. But what if it wasn't a cavity, I asked. I certainly didn't want to deal with another breakthrough, so I rejected that suggestion. Instead, I suggested that we push a fine wire through the pinhole to see if we could feel something on the other side. This we did. We pushed six inches of wire through the pinhole without touching anything. We were clearly through to the other side, but the audio quality was still terrible.

So we sat there scratching our heads, taking turns passing the earphones back and forth, listening to the muffled sounds from within the embassy building. We discussed all of the possibilities that would cause what we were hearing and decided that the most plausible reason was that we had drilled into a closet that had been added to the room. Unless the closet door were left open, this would account for the muffled audio. So we decided to drill yet another hole in the wall about five feet away from the first.

We worked well into the evening hours, and when the installation was complete, we pushed the microphone through the three-eighths-inch hole and seeded it up against the air passage. Unbelievably, we heard muffled sounds identical to those of the first installation. We were dumbfounded. We now had muffled audio in stereo!

After several weeks of monitoring, we determined that our targets had constructed a room-within-a-room for their most confidential briefings and discussions. This is actually a pretty standard security practice for many embassies around the globe. We just didn't expect it from this particular Asian embassy.

The United States, for example, uses a transparent Plexiglas structure nicknamed a "bubble" in most of its embassies. The bubble is actually a room large enough to hold a conference table and chairs of sufficient size to hold the embassy's entire country team. The bubble is assembled inside another room, which is shielded with copper coils so no transmissions can emanate from it. Therefore, anyone carrying an audio transmitter into the bubble would be unable to broadcast the signal to the outside. The fact that the bubble is constructed of transparent plastic also permits easy overall visual inspection, so if an audio device is somehow connected to it, it would be easily seen and disabled.

This particular room-within-a-room was certainly not that sophisticated, but it did prevent the type of audio penetration through a common wall that we were attempting.

The operation wasn't a total bust, however, because when meetings were held within the secret room, they often became very loud and animated, and these remarks were picked up by our stereo audio devices, despite the poor quality. The ambassador, in particular, had a loud, high-pitched voice that was very distinguishable and often reached our ears. In short, each time a meeting was held in the room, we were usually able to get enough complete sentences and phrases to know what topic was being discussed, what the main points of discussion were, and what the ambassador's opinion was. This was good intelligence.

So good in fact that the decision was made to penetrate all of the remaining rooms of the embassy to which we had access through the common wall, even though we had not yet determined their use. This involved yet another operation to gain access to the second-floor apartment of the apartment building. We accomplished this by furnishing the occupants with a student "au pair" who was on our payroll. Then, as soon as the occupants went out of town for a weekend, we entered the apartment and bugged the three remaining rooms sharing the common wall on the middle floor of the embassy. They turned out to be the ambassador's bedroom and two more offices, and they added significantly to the production of the entire operation.

A FINAL WORD ON AUDIO OPS

By this point, we were monitoring and recording eight separate audio installations in the embassy—the small salon and large salon on the first floor; the admin office, another staff office, and the secret room on the top floor; and the ambassador's bedroom and two more staff offices on the middle floor.

The operational information and intelligence produced by this single audio operation resulted in hundreds of pages of documents produced by the station every month. In addition to the staff officers working out of the station and at headquarters, it employed two full-time LP keepers and a half-dozen native transcribers-translators and their support staff.

Every word that was monitored and recorded at the LP had to be translated into English and transcribed. The raw transcriptions were then reviewed at the station, where case officers extracted all of the important operational information and reports officers extracted all of the intelligence information. The intelligence reports were then disseminated to a very select number of high government officials (including the White House and the national security adviser) on a strict "need to know" basis, and the operational information was sent back to headquarters, where it was further refined and either acted on or included in the appropriate operational files of the target officials.

In short, the handling of the material generated by this one audio operation involved a significant allocation of resources in and of itself. The work clearly doesn't stop when the bug is planted, and this is an important thing to remember whenever an audio operation is being considered, or when you suspect you are the victim of one.

AUDIO COUNTERMEASURES

As I mentioned at the beginning of the chapter, bugging of any sort is highly illegal unless it is done by a legitimate law enforcement agency with a court order in hand. But that does not deter unscrupulous private investigators working for big bucks on behalf of business competitors, or foreign governments, or hungry lawyers looking for dirt to support lawsuits, or disgruntled spouses looking for an advantage in a divorce proceeding, or political parties in desperate need of opposition research on a candidate, or even insurance agencies fighting an insurance claim from taking the risk of contracting an illegal audio penetration operation.

The sale and installation of illegal audio surveillance devices is a multibillion-dollar industry in the United States alone. Desperate people will go to great lengths, even at the risk of breaking the law, to achieve their goals. And any person or any entity with money, power, influence, or sensitive information worth stealing is at risk of being bugged.

WARNING SIGNS

Let's assume for a moment you fall into one of the categories mentioned above. How would you know you are being bugged? What would be some of the warning signs that could indicate you have become the target of an illegal eavesdropping operation?

If you are a businessman, you may become aware that your competitors appear to know more than they should about your company's plans, products, or other trade secrets than they should, or perhaps proprietary information is being suspiciously leaked to the press or stock market analysts. At first you may ask yourself if this is only a coincidence. Well maybe it is. However, it may not be.

There are other telltale signs. You may notice strange sounds like static, popping, or scratching on your phone lines. Weird sounds may even be coming from your phone when it is still on the hook, or the phone may ring often without anyone being on the line when you pick up the receiver. Your AM/FM radio or television may develop interference problems that were not there before. Or there may be visual signs of a technical penetration, like strange water staining on a wall or ceiling, or plaster dust under a wall outlet that may also be ajar. You may have been visited by repairmen (television, cable, and so forth) who claimed to be looking for some sort of a problem, but who were not called by you. Or a van or delivery truck has been suspiciously parked on the street in front of your home or office for several days. What do you do if you notice one or more of these telltale signs? Chalk it up to paranoia and forget about it? Call the police or telephone company? The answer is: none of the above.

WHAT TO DO IF YOU THINK YOU ARE BEING BUGGED

If you think you are being bugged, first of all, remain calm and think for a minute. Are you really being paranoid or would someone actually benefit in some rather large way by listening in on your phone conversations or eaves-dropping on your meetings in your office, home, car, or boardroom? If the answer is an unequivocal yes, then you must take action to determine whether you actually are being bugged, and if so, to find out who is behind the operation. The latter question is usually pretty easy to figure out; it's finding the bug that may be the difficult part. The difficulty of detection is directly related to the professionalism of the person who engineers the audio operation. In short, if a professional organization like the FBI or the CIA is behind the operation, you probably won't be able to find any evidence at all; but if a local private investigator (PI) was hired to plant the bug, a professional TSCM (Technical Surveillance Countermeasures) technician will more than likely be able to locate it and remove it. It simply depends on the sophistication of the plant and the equipment used.

So you have noticed some of the telltale signs and you feel strongly that a competitor or other form of adversary could benefit from an audio surveillance operation directed at you or your company. The first thing to do is to get away from the areas where you might be vulnerable (home, office, auto, and so forth) and to a phone that is not connected in any way with you or your company. A pay phone or a friend's home phone will usually do just fine. Never, ever use one of your own phones to discuss your suspicions with anyone. Doing so could immediately alert the individuals who are listening in to your conversations, allowing them to take action to remove or turn off their audio devices until the technical sweep is completed, and then to turn them back on again after the technician's departure. Then, from that outside phone, call a competent TSCM technician and set up an appointment to discuss your problem.

But you must beware of charlatans; the TSCM industry is full of them. They are called "raindancers" in the trade, because they will sweep through your premises waving a wand attached to some sort of black box and then charge you an extraordinary fee for their services. These raindancers are also known for planting their own bugs while they are doing their hocus-pocus, and then ostensibly finding them to ensure repeat business. These are the worst ones. Others are simply incompetent and lack the training and (very expensive) electrical equipment that are required to do a proper TSCM inspection.

A visit to the Granite Island Group's website (http://www.tscm.com) is an excellent way to learn more about what a TSCM sweep entails and to obtain a list of some of the real professionals in the industry. The Granite Island Group's James Atkinson estimates that there are only about a dozen legitimate and competent TSCM counterintelligence specialists working in the U.S. private sector. This may be a bit of an exaggeration, but the point is well taken. It takes years of training and experience to produce a qualified TSCM technician, and the best training ground is still the U.S. government's counterintelligence agencies. So, a good rule of thumb when selecting a TSCM specialist to do your sweep is to ask where he or she worked before entering the private sector. If the specialist can't answer with a minimum of ten years of experience in the trade with the CIA, FBI, NSA, State Department, or Defense Intelligence Agency (DIA), I wouldn't hire the person. Also, be prepared to spend between $2,000 and $5,000 a day for the services of a TSCM tech. These guys don't come cheap.

TYPES OF LISTENING DEVICES

Bugs can be implanted in almost anything. The only limiting factor is size. The host must be large enough to hold a microphone at the minimum, and unless there is a power source (for example, an AC line) to tap into, it must be large enough to carry a sufficient supply of batteries as well. Despite great advances in battery technology, miniaturization still presents problems, especially if battery life is to be extended over several weeks or months. Then, in most cases, a transmitter will be required as well, which takes up some more room in the host concealment. And then we may want to add a switch so that we can turn the device on and off to conserve battery power and add an additional layer of security to the device. You see where this is leading. The bugged olive in the martini is pure fiction. The host concealment must not only be large enough to contain a sufficient supply of batteries along with the microphone, transmitter, and possibly a switch, but it must also be something that will be placed where useful conversations are held. We discussed this in the section on Trojan horse concealments. So, if a competitor gives you a fancy desktop pen set, beware. It may be transmitting all of your most confidential office conversations to a recorder in a nearby listening post. The TSCM technician will want to examine all such gifts, as well as other possible hosts in your most vulnerable locations.

He will examine (and possibly X-ray) anything that he suspects could be a host or concealment for an audio device. He will look for pinholes in the walls and may even remove baseboards, particularly near electrical outlets, to check for hidden bugs. He will pay particular attention to lamps, clocks, and other electrical devices (remember the multiple plug adapter we discussed earlier?) that could serve as convenient hosts with their own supply of AC current. He will pay particular attention to RF transmissions that might come from a hidden audio device. To do this, he will monitor all suspected frequencies with sophisticated IPM (In-Place Monitoring) radio equipment. These sophisticated receivers are able to identify RF emanations from bugs even if they are hidden or masked behind normal frequencies. More special equipment is used to check all of the electrical wiring and telephone lines in the room for hidden devices.

WIRETAPPING

This is the area where the victim is most vulnerable. Wiretapping, most commonly tapping into phone lines, is the preferred method of most PIs and police organizations. The reason is simple: it's easy and does not usually require direct access to the room or phone instrument being bugged. The method only involves tying into a telephone line or other wire conductor that is used for communications (PBX cable, video or alarm system, and so forth), and listening in from some remote location. In the case of telephones (the most common), physical access is gained to the target line at some point between the main telephone company switching station and the target home or office, and a second set of wires is attached to the target pair to bridge the signal back to a listening post. If this is accomplished at the phone company, it won't be found. But if it is accomplished at any other junction box or spot on the line between there and the target, it may be found by the TSCM technician. Often a transmitter is installed at the point of the tap to broadcast the data to a nearby listening post. The transmitter adds to the security of the operation by permitting the eavesdropper to monitor the conversations from a remote location, but the RF signal it produces also increases the chances that it will be detected by a qualified TSCM tech. The alternatives—live monitoring or installing a tape recorder at the point of the tap (usually inside a junction box)—are much less secure. In short, it is easy for someone to access your phone lines, and even an amateur PI can tap a phone line. All that is required is for the eavesdropper to walk up to one of the many (often unlocked) distribution boxes linked to the target, identify the correct phone pair, and twist on a couple of wires connected to a tape recorder or transmitter. A competent PI who has done his homework to identify the correct phone lines can accomplish the actual installation in a matter of seconds.

MORE ON THE TELEPHONE

When I was serving in Hong Kong, I remember one of my senior CIA colleagues saying that he was going to retire at the end of his current tour. I tried to talk him out of it because I liked him personally and because he was such a good manager and case officer. He just looked at me and said: "You know, Fred, there comes a time in every case officer's life when he just gets tired of leaving his air-conditioned office and walking downtown in the heat to use a pay phone when there is a perfectly good instrument sitting right there on his desk." I could only nod. Been there, done that.

The telephone is a great communication tool. We couldn't conduct business without it today. It's also the most vulnerable instrument in our possession. So, if you don't want your enemies or competitors to know your plans, don't discuss them over the telephone. Period! By the way, that includes faxes and e-mail. Nothing that passes over a phone line is secure, unless (perhaps) it is encrypted. This fact is fairly well known; what isn't so well known is that your telephone not only can be tapped to record phone conversations, but it also easily can be turned into an active audio device that will pick up and transmit all conversations that take place within twenty feet of the phone, even when the phone is on the hook. Let me repeat that: all of your conversations in the room, regardless of whether you are speaking into the telephone, can be picked up and recorded by an eavesdropper. You see, telephones have built-in microphones, power, and speakers that provide everything an eavesdropper needs to listen in on your conversations. Modems, speaker phones, and cordless and cell phones also emit RF energy that can be easily intercepted by an eavesdropper using an inexpensive police scanner.

In some cases, nothing has to be done to the phone to turn it into an active audio device; in others it only takes the installation of a simple capacitor to enable an eavesdropper to listen in on all of your phone and room conversations. An RF transmitter can be added to broadcast the signal to a remote location, and power can be obtained from the current already on the phone line, tapped from a nearby AC line or from a small battery that can easily be attached.

A TCSM technician can advise you about the most vulnerable phone systems and whether someone has planted something in your phone or on your phone line. He will conduct a thorough inspection of every vulnerable telephone instrument with the aid of sophisticated electronic test equipment that will tell him whether the existing electronic characteristics of the telephone instrument and the associated wiring have been modified in any way. One simple and effective precaution against any form of phone tapping is to unplug your phone when it is not in use. This is done routinely by CIA officers stationed abroad, who are highly vulnerable to this type of bugging operation. You must, of course, still remember not to say anything you don't want broadcast to others when the phone is in use, because once the phone is plugged in, all of the above applies once again.

6

COMPUTER DATABASES
AND THE INTERNET

There is no question that the advent of the Internet and the computer revolution of the past twenty years have brought about a tremendous change in the way we access information and what information is publicly available. In the not so distant past, a very limited number of information databases were available to the general public—fee-based or not—and the ones that were available were generally complex and difficult to use, not to mention very expensive. Without a centralized repository to tap into, an investigator or research analyst had to visit the library or courthouse personally and spend countless hours digging through 3x5 cards and other files and records to find the information they were looking for.

Even repositories that have long been accessible, like the Library of Congress, which houses every book published in the United States and tons of other useful documents and publications, were not available to the researcher without a personal visit. Once in the library, the researcher would have to locate the book or documents needed, wait for the librarians to retrieve them, and then manually flip through the pages to search for the information desired. A library or courtroom visit would often turn into an all-day affair.

Things have changed drastically over the past decade. Now a computer-competent researcher with the right equipment can log on to the Internet and download volumes of useful information on a variety of subjects.

The advent of the personal computer, combined with the exponential increase of data readily available on the Internet and on subscriber-based information databases, has revolutionized the way we research today, and it has changed the information-gathering and investigative industries forever.

The cybersleuth has all but replaced the gumshoe; private investigators who are not computer literate and who cannot (or will not) invest in the databases now available simply cannot compete with modern investigators. The ex-cop gumshoe PI is indeed a dying breed.

THE GREAT DATABASE IN THE SKY

In the past decade, the information revolution has gone so far the other way that the problem now is taming the information beast; more and more of it is coming on line every day, and there is a lot of garbage among the nuggets. There are literally thousands of database and Internet resources, and knowing where to look for what information is a constantly changing and challenging task.

This onslaught of information resources begs the question of what is out there to tap into, and what is not available from a desktop computer.

One of the great fallacies that has spread rapidly over the past several years, mainly through fictional Hollywood movies, is the myth that somewhere out in cyberspace there is a "Great Database in the Sky"—a huge central repository that can be tapped into and, voilà, instant answers appear miraculously on your computer screen. These people may also believe that, since the Internet is a free service, they can get instant access to any information they want for no cost.

Not so! Not only is there no single repository for everything you want to know, but there also is very little out there of any significance that is "free."

For example, those of you with an e-mail account have probably received junk mail proclaiming to give you access to a database that will allow you to "Find Out Anything on Anyone!" This is a perfect example of an Internet scam that preys on the unenlightened. The fact is, there is no database in the world that will let you find out everything on anyone. Period. And if there were, do you really think you'd be able to access it for only $29.95 a month?

The Internet is a repository of public information, and most of that information is posted by people and companies that want you to know about them. It's a form of advertising. The information, therefore, may be exaggerated or misleading, because there are no controls over the accuracy of it, and as we well know, people are prone to try to present themselves in the best light possible, even if they have to fib a little.

Today, anyone can be "BillGates@aol.com" or can put up a website that states that their company has hundreds of employees, offices in twenty different countries, and revenues of over a billion dollars. Not every company that posts a slick website can be presumed to be legitimate. It's an old saying, but things are not always what they appear.

SEARCHING THE INTERNET AND DATABASES

Although databases are not the end all for the investigator, there is a tremendous amount of information out there on line that is available to the researcher at the stroke of a key. One of the best investigative database researchers in the country, Teri Rustmann of CTC International Group, will take us through the process.

Computer databases come in two forms: fee based and free. And since most information providers realize that information has value, they are not about to give it away for free if they can sell it. With that said, free is always a good place to start to search for what you want, because the less time spent searching on the fee-based databases the more money you will save.

So the first step is to log on to the Internet, where you can search away and collect all that you can for no cost. When trying to find a person, for example, there are some decent Internet-based locator services: http://www.anywho.com, http://www.411locate.com, http://www.555-1212.com, and http://www.whowhere.com are all good places to find a phone number or an address. For information on the U.S. government information network, including government websites and unclassified reports, go directly to http://www.fedworld.gov. The site contains databases on everything from Supreme Court decisions to foreign news to descriptions of 10,000 U.S. government files and U.S. federal job announcements. The website also contains information on the U.S. Customs Service and on more than 17,000 trade-related documents that can help a company do business internationally. In the site's National Technical Information Service (NTIS) Technical Reports database, you will find a title listing of 370,000 U.S. government reports published over the past ten years. Many of these and other reports can be downloaded to your computer in their entirety, but a fee is charged for this additional service, which gets us back to the "information has value" premise we discussed earlier.

There are also more and more public records coming on line. For instance, many states now have secretary of state sites where you can search for corporate registrations, and the U.S. SEC has a very good site where you can search for public filings on a company for free—something that used to be very costly to access through fee-based databases.

Some newspapers will now let you search their archives for free, although most of them still charge some kind of fee. And of course, you can always search for a website, which will give you a good starting point on the structure and nature of a company. It usually will also give you the names and some biographic data on its principle officers.

As long as you keep in mind that anybody with a little bit of computer knowledge can create and post a website and that there is no oversight authority to require that the information on the site must be true, you can still benefit from the information provided, and it is an ideal place to begin almost any research project. At a minimum, there are usually little bits of information that will provide you with leads to search for additional details.

For example, there usually will be a physical address on the website, and, if that address is near you, a simple walk by will tell you whether the office is legitimate or a Mail Boxes Etc. letter drop. And once you have the proper name and address of a company, you can begin looking for a corporate registration and past litigation, among other things.

INFORMATION BROKERS

Some of the best on-line databases act as information brokers by reselling information sold to them by licensing agencies like state motor vehicle departments, credit reporting agencies, and many others. They enable an investigator to obtain social security numbers, dates of birth, past and present addresses, corporate affiliations, the names of neighbors and relatives, and other public records, including information on liens, bankruptcies, civil judgments; marriage and divorce records; property records; and information on professional licenses.

They are almost always fee based, and some of the better ones, like Database Technologies, ChoicePoint, and Loc8fast, can get quite expensive. There also are a slew of smaller information companies that are popping up every day, increasing competition, which, in turn, tends to drive prices down.

I should hasten to add, however, that the very existence of these on-line information brokers is currently in jeopardy because of an ongoing legal battle with right-to-privacy advocates concerning the right to disseminate this kind of personal information. As a form of compromise, most of these databases are not available to the general public; access to them is limited to licensed private investigators, law firms, and other government-regulated users. We'll go into this in more depth further on in the chapter.

PERSONAL INFORMATION DATABASES

Regardless of whether this kind of personal information should be made available to the general public, in the right hands it is an invaluable tool for developing good intelligence for a background check on an individual or a company due-diligence investigation. The resulting information is put to good use by companies and individuals to weed out the crooks and charlatans who may otherwise penetrate their lives and livelihoods. The importance of knowing the ethical and moral standards of the people you are about to be dealing with cannot be overstated.

Fortunately, more and more databases are coming on line that will help to establish a picture of the person with whom you're about to enter into some sort of a relationship.

For example, the American Medical Association (AMA) now has a database where you can check out the credentials of doctors. The State of Florida has taken this a step further and recently established a site through its Division of Licensing that not only posts information on doctors' medical degrees and backgrounds, but also includes a listing of complaints that have been filed against them. (Not surprisingly, when this was first proposed, the doctors who complained the loudest were the same ones who had the most complaints logged against them. Those with clean records didn't seem to mind at all.) Other states post similar information.

The Martindale Hubble directory provides basic background information on lawyers, and a visit to the National Association of Securities Dealers (NASD) database will let you check out your stockbroker's record.

Of course, once again, there are caveats. Not all doctors are members of the AMA, lawyers have to pay to be registered with Martindale Hubble, and the NASD database only lists brokers who have been active within the last two years. So none of these databases are comprehensive, and your target may not appear at all (which doesn't necessarily mean she's a fraud). But these and other similar databases are good starting places to obtain basic information on professionals.

There also are databases that let you search for litigation, providing information on past civil and criminal lawsuits involving individuals and companies. Lexis, Westlaw, Courtlink, and Pacer are some of the best known. These databases will help you find out whether an individual or a company has been involved in civil or criminal litigation (including arrests and convictions), and will usually tell you what the nature and result of the litigation was.

Before these databases became available (in the not so distant past), the researcher would first have to identify where the litigation took place, and then physically go to the courthouse and do a hand search of the public records. Now, you can pull up the citation you are looking for with a few clicks right from your own desktop computer.

The bad news is that subscriptions to these databases are generally very expensive and they are relatively complicated to use, which severely hampers their usefulness for all but private investigators, law firms, and the like.

Another drawback is that they are not comprehensive; not all court records in all counties in all states are yet available, so the chance remains that you might miss something. In addition, they don't usually give you the entire history or disposition of a case. For the most part, you will only learn that your target was involved in a certain kind of dispute on a certain date, and the disposition of the case. Details of what actually happened will usually not appear. However, with the case number, you can then go to the courthouse and pull the file to get the full story.

PRESS SOURCES

Other invaluable database resources in the researcher's arsenal include the various press databases such as Nexis, Dialog, and DowJones. They are some of the best, but again, they are expensive. There are, however, some less expensive alternative sources coming on line every day. One of them, http://www.elibrary.com, while not nearly as extensive as the fee-based databases, is only a fraction of the cost, so it's a good place to start when running a press search.

When collecting business intelligence, press is one of the most reliable, efficient, and cost-effective ways to find information on a subject. The information is available at a keystroke, and it's usually pretty reliable. Journalists generally have to check out their stories fairly thoroughly before they go to print, especially journalists from well-known publications like *Newsweek,* the *New York Times,* and the *Washington Post.*

The main problem with searching press is the sheer volume of information that is available. The trick here is not to look at a general subject, but to narrow the search to the bare essentials. It can always be expanded later on, if necessary.

Let's say, for example, you are looking for competitive intelligence on the telecommunications industry in Brazil. You could try searching "telecommunications" and "Brazil," but that would net you somewhere around 20,000 hits—not a manageable amount of information. So you have to begin to narrow the search. You might want to start with the time frame—you're only interested in current information, not anything historical, so you can still search "telecommunications" and "Brazil," but specify that you are only interested in publications for the current year. Next, since you may only really be interested in problems that other companies have encountered with the Brazilian government, you could now add to the search string terms like "litigation" or "lawsuit" or maybe "Brazilian Government." If it's still unmanageable, you might want to exclude some words—"not AT&T," for example, until you come up with a workable number of core articles that will give you substantive bits and pieces of information that an analyst can turn into finished intelligence.

A final word of caution on press: As with all other database information, not everything you read in the paper is true. Even highly respectable publications have been fooled. For example, a few years ago the highly respected *Forbes Magazine* ran a cover story on a supposed business turnaround expert and entrepreneur extraordinaire. It later came out that the expert was a long-time con artist with a long criminal record, including convictions for fraud, embezzlement, and misrepresentation. *Forbes* later retracted the story and admitted that even they had been terribly fooled, but if an analyst doing a background investigation on the subject had stopped with just the *Forbes* article, she would have provided her client a terribly flawed and inaccurate intelligence report. So the moral of the story is: Always get the whole story, and don't believe everything you read in the press—or anywhere else for that matter.

INACCURATE INFORMATION

Much of the information on the various databases, Internet based or not, may also be inaccurate. Just because someone found something on a database does not mean the information is correct. This goes back to the difference between information and intelligence. Very rarely does one piece of information tell a whole story, and anyone who makes a decision based on only one piece of a puzzle is not a very good decision maker.

For example, inexperienced investigators will often suspect fraud when they come upon more than one social security number attached to an individual they are tracing. They immediately jump to the conclusion that if an individual is using a "second" social security number, he must be trying to assume a second identity to conceal something; an obvious indication of criminal intent. Sounds logical, but is it?

The answer is: not necessarily. It's true that people can and do obtain different social security numbers for fraudulent purposes, but before jumping to any conclusion, the investigator should first rule out the possibility that the other social security number may belong to a spouse (married couples often have social security numbers show up on each others records), or to a child (is the parent a custodian for an account?), or, the most common reason of all, simply a data entry error (for example, the lady with the long fingernails at the Department of Motor Vehicles hit the wrong key when inputting the applicant's registration information).

This is particularly true when the second social security number is just one digit off from the original number. Although bad guys can and do frequently change a digit or two to try to obfuscate their identity, it is not at all uncommon for a 4 to be transcribed as a 9 or for the number that appears directly above the correct number on a numeric keypad to appear in place of the real one (4 instead of 1, 5 instead of 2, 6 instead of 3, and so on). Remember the long fingernails.

Also, it is a good rule never to overlook the obvious, whether tracing a person on computer databases or conducting any form of investigation, or in life for that matter. When you are driving down the highway and your car starts to sputter and stall, the first place to look is at the gas gauge. Only when it doesn't read "empty" should you begin thinking about a blown engine.

CROSS CHECK AND DOUBLE CHECK

Database information can be correct, incorrect, misleading, sketchy, complete, incomplete, nonexistent, or invaluable. Perhaps the most perplexing scenario is when the database researcher obtains partial information on a subject and some clues that indicate there is more to the story, but the critical information that should be there simply doesn't appear.

This happened in a recent case when we were doing a background investigation on an individual who was arranging financing for a client. The client wanted to make sure that the investor was legitimate and that he had the ability to fulfill the terms of the financing that he claimed. The fact that the fellow was asking for money up front to obtain the financing also caused the client some degree of alarm. (We will discuss this type of "advance fee" fraud in great depth in the chapter on corporate and financial fraud.)

Although several red flags popped up early in the investigation to indicate the investor was not the financial heavy hitter he purported to be, there was nothing concrete. Mainly, he just didn't meet the profile of a successful investor, and we suspected there was something we were missing.

Then, during a personal interview with a former associate of the investor, we learned that the investor had previously been convicted in Connecticut on felony charges related to running an advance fee scheme. This was startling news, because we suspected this was the very thing he might be trying to do with the client, but nothing had turned up during our initial database search—according to the database records, the investor had no criminal record in Connecticut or anywhere else in the United States.

So the scramble was on to find the case file and obtain the details. We again searched every county in Connecticut but came up with the same result: nothing. We even looked at all the adjacent states with the same negative results. Either our source was misinformed and there was no felony conviction, or the databases were wrong.

Frustrated, we turned to an FBI contact who specialized in running down advance fee scheme perpetrators. We provided him with all of the information we had acquired on the subject, told him the story of the felony conviction mystery, and asked for his help in getting to the bottom of the matter.

The first thing he checked was the NCIC (National Crime Information Center) database. (The database contains all criminal arrests and convictions reported in the United States, but is only available to law enforcement officers—private investigators and other nongovernment officials are not permitted access to it.)

Although he was unable to give us the details, he was clearly reading the NCIC record of the case on his computer screen. He advised us to look again in Connecticut, and we did, with the same result. He then told us to look at a specific county in Connecticut, and we did again, with the same negative result. Frustrated and unable to tell us what he was reading on his computer screen, he then instructed us to send someone to the county courthouse where, clearly, according to the NCIC, the conviction had been handed down and recorded. Unbelievably, we had a court researcher check the courthouse, but the same negative result was reported.

We then went back to our FBI source and pleaded with him to tell us what was going on. Why hadn't the conviction shown up during our database search, and above all, why was there no mention of it at the courthouse? It couldn't just be a computer glitch where the data had inadvertently not been entered into the system, or perhaps had been erroneously deleted, because there was no record of the conviction at the courthouse either.

Now totally frustrated, our FBI friend went back into the NCIC database and a deeper check revealed that all records of the case had been expunged (not just sealed) as part of the defendant's plea bargain agreement. In other words, in return for a plea of guilty for running the advance fee scheme, the investor's attorney had arranged for the entire record of the case to be expunged from the court records for all eternity.

No mention of the case remained in the public domain. All that remained was the NCIC notation. Unbelievable!

That's why the crook felt confident enough to return to his old tricks and resume cheating unsuspecting clients. With the smug arrogance of a professional thief, he even used the exact same fraudulent advance fee scheme that he had been arrested and convicted for a few years earlier. He knew with assurance that a routine background check by a private investigative firm would never uncover evidence of his past deeds.

So here we had a convicted felon on the loose, again perpetrating an identical illegal scam for which he had already once been arrested and punished, and yet there were no available public records on the case.

Unfortunately, as we later learned, certain states are known for sealing or expunging records if there is a guilty plea bargain, and Connecticut is one of them. So, in this particular case, no routine criminal check from a database would ever have turned up anything on the scam artist. It took a human source to provide the lead to the information we were seeking and a friendly FBI source who was willing to bend the rules a bit in the interest of justice and fairness to the unsuspecting client to confirm the negative information.

Anything that is publicly available must be independently verified in order to validate it's accuracy. There are more than a few examples of criminal cases that most people would never find through a normal search of public records for a myriad of reasons, including typographical errors or the misspelling of the criminal's name. So always be thorough and check and double check, and never believe something is or isn't true just because it came from a database.

THE RIGHT-TO-PRIVACY ISSUE

As noted earlier, the right-to-privacy advocates are lobbying hard to limit or stop any of this kind of personal information from being made available at all. They argue that individual privacy rights are more important than the rights of employers and others who believe they have a right to know what sort of person they are about to hire, or do business with, or marry. Clearly, it's a difficult and emotional issue.

Certainly, everybody is entitled to a certain amount of privacy, and few will disagree that the behavior by the paparazzi in the Princess Diana and other celebrity cases has gone too far. Photographers shouldn't be permitted to peer into bedroom windows with telephoto lenses or to otherwise invade the sanctity of one's home. These invasive acts clearly overstep the bounds of common decency and, indeed, the law.

The principle that guides the law in cases like these is that every individual has a "reasonable expectation of privacy." The debate centers on the word *reasonable.* In some cases, it is clear-cut, but in others, it's not so clear-cut. For example, an employer has the right to place video cameras in office and warehouse spaces to deter theft and malingering, but not in the restrooms. Similarly, a private investigator running a trash operation on a residence is free to grab someone's trash after the trash container has been placed in the street for pickup by the garbage collectors, but not while it's still on the person's property. In both cases, the "reasonable expectation of privacy" rule applies (as well as trespass in the trash example).

But if a company or individual is about to invest several million dollars in a new company, do they have the right to know who they are dealing with? Do they have the right to know if any of the principals have criminal records; or if their claims of business experience and education degrees are true; or if the chief financial officer of the company has been fired from his last three jobs for incompetence and embezzling funds?

Convicted felons give up their right to vote in the United States. Should these same persons have the right to have the conviction records sealed or expunged? What about the rights of those people who want to know with whom they are dealing?

WHEN THE PC IS USELESS

Sometimes you may know where the answer to a question may lie, but the information is inaccessible through the Internet or computer databases.

A recent example of this occurred when a client (let's call him Paul), who had been defrauded out of more than $250,000 in an offshore investment scheme, wanted to know the names of the other investors in the fund so that he could contact them about putting together some kind of class action suit to attempt to recover some of the money.

We told Paul there were probably two places where the investors would be listed: the fund managers would have a list, and the fund's liquidating agent, Ernst & Young, would have a list.

Paul's immediate reaction was: "Great! Now all you have to do is hack into their computers and download the lists." We explained to him that "hacking" was not an option, because it was illegal. Also, since the information was held only within the two companies and perhaps their accounting firms, it would not appear on any public database. So we would have to look elsewhere for the information.

In the end, we were able to obtain the list of investors for Paul, but the information was obtained through a human source who was involved in the liquidation of the fund, not from any database.

COMBINING DATABASE AND HAND SEARCHING

In a recent case involving a sizable inheritance, the family patriarch died after setting up a trust fund for his family. His will stated that his assets would be distributed through the fund equally to his two children, a son and a daughter, and subsequently to their children, and their children, and so on.

Many years later, the patriarch's homosexual son, a man who had never married, died and passed on his portion of the trust to a person whom he claimed was his son. The patriarch's daughter, who was now married with children of her own, questioned the legitimacy of the claim. She argued that her homosexual brother would never have fathered a child, and in any event, he would have been only fourteen years old when the child was born. She claimed that the "son" was, in fact, her brother's lover, who did not qualify to benefit from the family trust fund.

The surprise came when the "son" produced a birth certificate that appeared to establish that he was indeed the brother's natural son. The family was flabbergasted.

The fact remained, if this individual were indeed the patriarch's legitimate grandson, then he would have a legal right to his father's portion of the trust.

It was at this point that we were contacted by the family's lawyer and asked to try to sort out the puzzle and determine if it was at all possible that this person could be the patriarch's grandson.

The key bit of evidence in the case was located in an obscure little book sitting on a dusty shelf in the Library of Congress. It was written and published (only twenty copies were printed) by the "grandson's" uncle, and contained a genealogical history of the entire family. Among other things, it outlined in great detail the family history, including the birth of the "grandson" himself and the names of his natural parents (which did not include the homosexual son of the patriarch).

The existence of the book was found in a citation during an Internet search of the "grandson's" family, but the brief citation did not include any details of the family tree. It took a personal visit to the Library of Congress by a researcher to retrieve and copy pages from the actual book to obtain the necessary information.

The ability to search from a PC and access the citation in the first place was the key lead that told us where to find definite proof of the fake grandson's lineage.

But what about the birth certificate that was produced by the imposter grandson? If this individual was not the homosexual son's biological son, how did he acquire a birth certificate showing him to be an offspring? Was the certificate a forgery? Not entirely. Since the two had been a couple for a very long time, the patriarch's son wanted to ensure that his lover would be taken care of after his death. However, given the strict terms of the trust, the son would have to be very creative to make sure his lover would benefit. So, he legally adopted his lover and had the lover's real birth certificate altered to reflect that he was a natural-born son.

The case is still in litigation.

THE MIND-SET OF THE DATABASE RESEARCHER

So, how does one go about making sense of all the information that is now available? There is a prodigious amount of information available to anyone who knows how to extract it, but it takes a special skill to search and cull through the volumes of public information available today.

There are two issues to keep in mind when searching for information in databases: first is having the knowledge and the skill to find and then extract the public information that is available; and second, if the information is not publicly available, then you need to be able to use the public information you find to give you clues that will lead you to the not-so-public information.

Here is an illustration of the first issue. Several years ago a client, a large hotel chain, was looking to go into a partnership with a Canadian investor to build a new hotel. The client wisely decided to do a background check on the individual before moving forward with the deal.

At first blush, the investor looked fine. Civil and criminal traces came back negative, and a Dun & Bradstreet report stated that the subject's company had eighty-six employees and an annual gross sales of $50 million.

But then a few inconsistencies in the subject's background started showing up. As we continued to dig deeper, we found that the man's name was not Robert Mapelwood (I have changed the name here for the purposes of illustration) as he gave it to our client, but was actually Robert Maplewood, and under his real name he was wanted in the United States on fraud and embezzlement charges. Additionally, his company (the one with the favorable D&B) did not exist. The address he provided, which was in a very good section of London, did not exist either.

The client was astounded, but acknowledged that they had thought it strange that the investor would never meet with them in the United States and had always insisted that their meetings take place in Canada. Needless to say, the client did not go through with the deal, and the intelligence they obtained saved them from making a terrible business decision.

This is typical in many fraud cases. Perpetrators often will make a small spelling change to their names or transpose a few letters. They also often use a name, particularly a company name, that is very similar to a large, legitimate company: something like "First Capital Advisers, Inc." They may also pick a legitimate company or banking institution and imply that they are affiliated with it: "We clear through Boston Securities and First Boston Bank." Well, they probably do have an account there, which is where they will deposit your money before they move it offshore.

It takes an experienced researcher to know when things look okay, and when, as in the case of Maplewood, you have to take it further. Often, things are simply not as they appear. That is why database research requires a certain mind-set—it takes more than simply running through the motions. If a researcher had taken Maplewood at face value, he would have been given a clean bill of health and the client would have been defrauded out of millions of dollars. Thoroughness is essential, as well as having keen instincts regarding what appears to be okay and what doesn't.

This is especially true when dealing with international cases and with foreign names that must be transliterated into English, like Arabic, Farsi, or Chinese. For example, take a name like Mohammed Ali-Akbar. How many ways do you think there are to spell Mohammed? The researcher must be aware that the name can be transliterated as Mohamed, Muhammed, or Mohahmed, to cite just a few examples. Checking all possible variations of the spelling could mean the difference in finding some crucial bit of information or missing it entirely.

So rule number one in name tracing is: check all possible variants.

The next thing to remember is that a good database exploiter will always keep digging and will trust her instincts to know when to keep looking and when she has acquired all that is out there. Looking to unearth that single nugget that will pull everything together can become an obsession that drives the best investigative researchers.

7

THE IMPORTANCE
OF ANALYSIS

Collection and analysis go together like ham and eggs. One is nothing without the other. But the role of the case officer and analyst, both of whom are professional intelligence officers, differs greatly. The case officer seeks answers to specific questions (intelligence requirements) through knowledgeable sources, and the analyst seeks the same answers through deductive reasoning after reviewing all of the available material on the subject.

In other words, the case officer tries to fill intelligence gaps by gathering precise nuggets of information, while the analyst tries to bridge these same gaps by making informed guesses based on what is known to be true and sound reasoning methods (if A plus B is equal to B plus C, then A must be equal to C). The symbiosis is very real, and the coordination process between the two disciplines is dynamic.

Following is an example of faulty analysis caused by the paucity of precise, current information from knowledgeable sources.

WHITHER HONG KONG: PURE CONJECTURE

During a four-year stint in Hong Kong back in the late 1970s, I was often called upon to brief visiting congressional delegations on the status of Hong Kong–China relations. One of the most frequently asked questions at the time was: What's going to happen to Hong Kong? The expectation was that, following the fall of Vietnam and the other Communist victories in Southeast Asia, China would redouble its efforts to return the colony to the motherland. The senators and congressmen wanted to know when the event was expected to take place.

With all of the smug self-importance of an experienced China watcher (but without the benefit of up-to-date information on the subject from reliable Chinese officials), I would proceed to pontificate to the groups on the history of the three treaties that legitimized Great Britain's occupation of the territory: The first gave the island of Hong Kong to Britain in perpetuity; shortly thereafter the second ceded a portion of the Kowloon Peninsula (directly across the harbor from Hong Kong Island) to the crown in perpetuity; and the third leased the surrounding "New Territories" to Britain for ninety-nine years.

I would then give the legislators my analysis of the situation, along with my prediction for the future, based solely on my historic deductions and a fair amount of knowledge about the Chinese character. I would explain to them that although the return of Hong Kong to China was both inevitable and foreseeable, the fact that none of the treaties was recognized by the current Chinese Communist government meant that the return would never take place when the ninety-nine-year lease treaty was due to expire on 1 July 1997.

I reasoned that it could occur before or after that date, but if it occurred on that exact date, it would imply tacit recognition by the Chinese government that the treaties did, in fact, exist, and this was something I believed China would never do. It was simply not in the Chinese character to do such a thing.

As events have shown, I was dead wrong. China can be very, very unpredictable, and my analysis was flawed from the beginning because it did not include the current thinking of the Chinese leadership on the subject. Despite being a case officer myself, I did not have current information from informed Chinese sources through the operations people—the case officers.

THE OTHER SIDE OF THE COIN

However, what is collection without analysis? Can the case officer work in a vacuum, without the support of the analysts? The answer is: it depends.

Remember the example I used in the chapter on recruitment concerning whether the lights were on or off in Hanoi following a B-52 raid? This intelligence requirement was very specific, but it was actually generated by intelligence analysts who wanted to know whether the main power plant had been hit. The fact that the lights were on after the raid was a pretty strong indication that the target had been missed. In this case, the spy answered the question and no analysis (other than the simple deduction that if the lights were on, the power grid was in operation) was required. Indeed, no amount of analysis could have answered this particular question. Under the circumstances—heavy cloud cover and the need to answer the question before the clouds cleared—only an observer, someone who was there, could tell whether the power plant had been hit during the raid.

The fact remains that only in very unique circumstances can the operations people or the analysts work in a vacuum, without the benefit of the other. Only in very rare instances can a source provide the whole picture; all of the facts and the analysis to boot. This is a luxury that does not occur with much frequency in the intelligence business, and it should not be expected.

Only when no sources are available to tap for specific new information should we rely solely on an analysis of old information to provide us with the answers; likewise, only when we are very fortunate or when the requirement is extremely narrow in scope should we rely solely on the operations people for the answers. Intelligence collectors and analysts should always work in concert with one another.

THE INTELLIGENCE PROCESS

Remember that intelligence is not just information; it is a circular process that involves several steps, and it essentially is a cycle that never actually ends. In the first step, the decision maker (for example, the president of a country or the CEO of a company) makes a request for information that will assist him in making a particular decision. This request is then sent down to the collectors, who, in turn, use whatever sources available to them to obtain information on that request. They may include searching databases containing press reports and other open-source information on the subject, direct interviews with individuals with access to the information desired, personal observation, human intelligence collection (interviews with sources using cover, access agents, or other clandestine methods), searching court records, and other information sources. All of the information collected in this exercise is called "raw intelligence," or "raw reporting."

Only after the raw information is reviewed, evaluated, collated, and written up in a coherent report for the decision maker is it called "finished intelligence." The finished intelligence report is then disseminated to the decision maker, who reads it, makes whatever decisions are called for on the basis of the new intelligence, and issues new requirements based on that new level of knowledge. This both completes the cycle and starts it off anew, with new requirements being generated and new information collected, analyzed, written up, and disseminated.

WHAT IS ANALYSIS?

The term "analysis" as used in the intelligence profession is somewhat of a misnomer. The process of analysis involves more than just analyzing and picking apart the information that has been collected; it is more a process of synthesizing and putting together all of the existing information that has been obtained on a particular topic and then examining it all to try to make sense out of it. After the analyst has read and understood the mound of raw information available to her, she looks at it critically to determine which pieces are most important, which are least important, and which may add flavor and understanding. The analyst must also filter each bit of information based on her general background knowledge on the subject to determine which of the information fits with other available data that is assumed to be true, and which doesn't. She must decide which information is probably correct, and which might be fabricated or simply wrong.

Then the analyst has the weighty responsibility of figuring out what it all means and what may happen as the result of that information. This is accomplished through some sort of reasoning process, usually through induction, deduction, abduction, or a combination of these methods. Only then can the information be put into final report format and disseminated to the consumer—the decision maker, who will take action based on the facts and analysis as they are presented.

WHY IS IT IMPORTANT?

Some people, including some case officers, question the need for analysts. They argue that the raw data does usually speak for itself and that the decision maker is perfectly capable of weighing the information, particularly after the collector—the case officer—has done his own analysis at the front end. Not so. The analysts play a critical role in the intelligence process by sifting through all the information, some of which is not available to the case officer in the field, putting all the important information in one place, providing context, and making sense out of it all in a thoroughly dispassionate manner.

In other words, raw data does not usually tell the whole story, and decision makers are generally far too busy to know every nuance of life in Ouagadougou or to plow through reams of paper trying to find out what kind of long-distance telephone service AT&T offers in Cuba or Belize.

WHAT, SO WHAT, AND WHY?

Former CIA analyst Lisa Ruth says the analyst approaches each project with three basic questions in mind: what? so what? and why? Sometimes the "what" is more important than the "so what" or the "why" is more important than the "what," and sometimes the question the decision maker really wants answered is actually "what next" or "how did that happen" or even "what if it rains during the offensive," but professional intelligence analysts tend to lump all of those questions into the what, so what, and why categories.

The purpose is to remind the analyst of the importance of adhering to rigorous analytical thought processes and to separate descriptions of events and phenomena from explanations of why they may have occurred and from estimations of what it all might mean for the future. But the analyst must be cautious not to go too far with their analytic judgments and estimations. Some analysts refer to this process as separating facts, findings, forecasts, and fortune-telling. Once the analyst moves from forecasting into fortune-telling, problems begin to arise.

The "what" is a statement of what happened, a statement of fact. It is a compilation of verified data directly related to the intelligence requirement. It is the reason the analyst is writing, and it is why the decision maker sends the requirement down to the collectors and analysts. It also provides the platform for the "so what" and the "why." In this portion of the intelligence report, the analyst seeks to present the facts as clearly and concisely as possible. This section must be completely objective, with no personal bias or conjecture attached. For example:

> IBM today announced it will lay off 200 employees over the next six years. The personnel cuts are the result of budget cutbacks resulting

from slow sales in the last half of 1999. According to the vice president for human resources, the cuts will primarily affect clerical and administrative positions, although she expects some cuts in the programming fields as well. The vice president further stated the majority of the job eliminations will come from retirement and other attrition.

Or

Overhead photography shows that Chinese troops are amassing along the Russian border, and more troops are moving from the interior to add extra strength to the force. More than sixty battalions have set up locations along the border since early yesterday evening, including infantry, tank, and heavy weapons units. Other troops from throughout the country have also begun to move toward the border. Satellite photography early this morning shows efforts by the military to camouflage equipment and personnel, both at the border and en route.

Once the facts are laid out concerning what happened (often, as in the China case, obtained from a reliable intelligence source), the follow-on intelligence requirement is generated and additional multisource information is collected to complete the picture. The analyst then puts all of this information together and tries to make sense out of it all; to answer the "so what" question. The analyst prepares a statement of findings that indicates what is increasing, decreasing, changing, or taking on a pattern and an interpretation of the significance of the events as they affect the larger picture.

In the IBM example, this would mean obtaining information on the background leading up to the decision to begin cutting staff, and then to see whether this was indicative of an overall pattern of staff cuts and other forms of pulling back and consolidating or an isolated occurrence. In the Chinese example, it would mean collecting information on the plans and intentions of the Chinese leadership vis-à-vis the Russians, and to cite indications concerning whether all of these troop movements were leading up to some sort of confrontation.

Finally, the analyst must answer the "why" question. Why is IBM laying off employees? Why is China moving troops along the Russian border? These forecasts must be made based on all of the facts and findings previously obtained, and they must be defended by sound and clear logical argumentation. They must not drift into the realm of fortune-telling, where inadequately explained and poorly defended judgments are offered.

SOURCE EVALUATION

The subject of source evaluation is so important to the analyst that it deserves special mention. As mentioned above, one of the major tasks of the analyst is to evaluate all of the bits of information that go into a finished intelligence report. That includes press reports (do you believe everything you read in the newspaper?), court records and other database information (data entry errors are common), and human sources.

I once had a professor named B. B. Chapman who taught Oklahoma history at Oklahoma State University. Professor Chapman was very big on the sourcing of information. In his mind, there were good historians and not so good historians, and he believed that the manner in which they reported historical incidents should be judged at least in part by their reputations as objective historians. In other words, some historians were more biased than others, and this bias would often show up in how they reported historical events.

So, every time he asked a question in class, he waited for the answer and then pointed to the student and pronounced in his deep, heavily accented Oklahoma drawl: "Your information's no better than your source!" The student would then have to relate where he obtained his information, and the class would evaluate the source as a way of proving or disproving the accuracy of the information.

This was a very important lesson that served me well during my years as an intelligence operations officer with the CIA. For example, when I was stationed in Hong Kong, I was tasked with the recruitment and handling of Hong Kong Chinese agents who had the ability to travel legally in and out of China on business or family visits. During the briefing sessions that preceded launching them on their missions onto the China mainland, I would review their tailored intelligence requirements and then talk with them about the importance of obtaining not only answers to the intelligence questions, but also the precise sourcing of their information.

I would explain that if they returned to Hong Kong and told me during the debriefing that a source told them the Chinese leader was seriously ill with lung cancer and had only a few months to live, that startling information would cause me to sit up in my chair. My next questions would be: "Who told you that? Who was the source of that information?"

If the agent were to answer: "Oh, I was in a cab in Beijing on my way to a cocktail reception and the cab driver told me," I might include the tidbit in my operational reporting as a rumor circulating Beijing, but it would never find its way into a field intelligence report.

However, if the agent were to say: "I was at a cocktail reception in Beijing and the Chinese leader's personal physician told me," I would be out of the door of the safehouse in an instant to rush back to the station to type up a blue-stripe, restricted handling, eyes only, flash precedence intelligence report that would go straight to the president of the United States and other senior government officials.

Same exact information, two different sources. The only difference was the sources' access to the information. The cab driver most likely did not have access to anyone with knowledge of the Chinese leader's health and was merely repeating a rumor he had heard on the street, while the physician had direct access to the Chinese leader and his health records.

Evaluating the sources of information is one of the most important tasks of the analyst. The chain of acquisition is especially important when evaluating human sources, because the closer one is to the ultimate source, the more accurate the reporting becomes. Other things, like past reporting reliability (Does the agent have a proven track record? Does he have a good memory?), and general truthfulness of the agent (Has the agent passed a polygraph examination recently? Has she passed other vetting tests of reliability?), are also important.

In the words of B. B. Chapman, "Your information's no better than your source."

THE INTELLIGENCE ANALYST

While the general perception of a case officer is of a swashbuckling, gregarious, outgoing James Bond type of individual, the analyst is perceived as the antithesis of this picture; this may be precisely why they need one another. One is the classic people-oriented extrovert, and the other a studious introvert. The case officer needs people skills in order to recruit and manipulate difficult agents, while the analyst must possess excellent reasoning skills and other cognitive attributes like written expression, reading, and oral comprehension; pattern recognition; and information ordering talents in order to pour through reams of disjointed documents and pieces of information and to make sense out of it all.

Research at the Joint Military Intelligence College demonstrates that professional intelligence analysts exhibit a pattern of personality traits that sets them apart from the U.S. population as a whole. The traits include preferring to work with ideas rather than things and people, gathering information through the senses rather than inspiration, making decisions based on logic rather than emotion, and a strong desire to find definite answers to problems rather than leaving possibilities open.

PERFECT SYMBIOSIS

The case officer and the analyst compliment one another in ways few other professionals do. They sit at both ends of the behavioral-personality scale and contribute equally to the intelligence process with their special skills. No company seriously involved in the work of business intelligence can do without both of them.

Part 3

INFORMATION PROTECTION AND COUNTERINTELLIGENCE

8

LEGAL ISSUES AND THE ECONOMIC ESPIONAGE ACT OF 1996

The FBI is aware of twenty-three countries currently conducting operations targeting U.S. trade secrets. It has been widely reported that France, for example, routinely bugged Air France flights and French hotel rooms to obtain economic and technical information from selected foreign passengers and guests. Three former directors of the DGSE, France's external security service, have publicly commented on France's prowess in conducting economic espionage. As recently as 1996, former DGSE director Claude Silberzahn said that in France "the state is not just responsible for law making, it is in business as well." He added: "For decades, the French state regulated the markets to some extent with its left hand while its right hand used the secret services to procure information for its own firms."

China has gone to similar lengths, as we will see in the next chapter. Vietnam and Cuba are aggressively following suit. Russia uses former KGB and GRU officers to collect information that will help the country compete more effectively in the global market as it struggles to create a free market economy. The energy that was once spent attempting to defeat the West during the cold war is now being devoted to gaining market share in the global marketplace. And traditional allies that are also strong economic competitors like Israel, Germany, Japan, Taiwan, and South Korea all actively target U.S. business information to gain a competitive edge internationally.

Futurist Alvin Toffler has said that corporate espionage will be one of the biggest businesses in the twenty-first century, which will be marked by information wars and increased economic and financial espionage. In a 1991 ruling, a U.S. federal judge stated that the nation's future largely depends on the efficiency of industry, and the efficiency of industry largely depends on the protection of industrial property.

The Economic Espionage Act (EEA) of 1996 was enacted to focus attention on the threat of foreign industrial spying and to give the federal government a mechanism to prosecute offenders. It allows the government to prosecute information theft whether it takes place in the United States, on the Internet, or in any international location. It was designed to cover the whole range of trade secrets, which are defined in the act as "information the owner has taken reasonable measures to keep secret," and information that "derives its economic value, actual or potential, from not being generally known to or available to the general public."

THE NEED FOR NEW LEGISLATION

The EEA was conceived after former FBI director Louis Freeh and others concluded that existing federal statutes simply did not allow the U.S. government enough clout to counter the growing threat of industrial espionage to the U.S. economy. In testimony before the Senate, Director Freeh said: "Intellectual property . . . government and corporate proprietary economic information, sustains the health, integrity, and competitiveness of the American economy and has been responsible for earning our nation's place in the world as an economic superpower."

While the United States may not be able to compete with some other countries in terms of low wages or natural resources, it does excel in ideas, inventiveness, research, and intellectual property development. IBM chairman Frank Cary drew a clear link between inventiveness and this country's economic well-being and standard of living when he said that when the reward of investment is destroyed, the incentive to innovate is also destroyed.

Intel Corporation's David Shannon provided a stunning example of this during a congressional hearing on the subject. He said: "Intel is a world class, sophisticated company with world class security . . . even though we have world class security and are very deeply involved in the computer industry . . . we recently were the victim of economic espionage where the value to the receiver of that information could range as high as $300 million."

In short, tens of billions of dollars and countless jobs were being lost, and the U.S. government was seemingly impotent in its efforts to counter it. It was hamstrung by having to use outdated statutes enacted long before the advent of computers, copy machines, and instant communications.

THE ADIRONDACK PROJECT

One of the more striking examples of the inadequacy of federal laws at the time occurred during the 1982 investigation of Hitachi's theft of information on IBM's highly classified "Adirondack" project. Adirondack was IBM's code name for its development of a new generation of mainframe computers. The information on the Adirondack program was literally worth billions of dollars to a competitor.

The FBI collected volumes of information regarding the theft, including some thirty-five hours of videotape showing damning evidence of meetings between an undercover FBI agent and an IBM undercover official's meetings with Hitachi officials. The tapes recorded the payment of $650,000 in bribe money given to the undercover officers by the Hitachi officials and detailed explanations given by them concerning the reasons why Hitachi wanted the IBM technology.

Hitachi entered a plea of guilty to the only thing they could be charged with at the time—conspiring to transport stolen IBM property to Japan—and was slapped on the wrist with the maximum penalty allowable under the law: $10,000.

Outraged, the FBI lobbied for new legislation to criminalize the theft of trade secrets. The result was the EEA of 1996.

THE ECONOMIC ESPIONAGE ACT

The Economic Espionage Act of 1996 was passed to protect U.S. companies from efforts by foreign governments or companies to steal U.S. technology and proprietary information. The FBI director highlighted the need for the new legislation by saying that foreign espionage against U.S. businesses was a real and growing threat. The EEA was enacted with two goals in mind: to thwart attempts by foreign entities to steal our trade secrets, and to allow the federal government to investigate and prosecute all offenders, including foreign information thieves and domestic American competitors. The act included cybercrimes and illicit duplication of intangible trade secrets. In short, it updated the law for the new millennium.

The act focused attention on economic espionage and gave the federal government the mechanism to prosecute offenders. Under the act, the theft of trade secrets, defined as "all forms of financial, business, scientific, technical, economic, or engineering information . . . if the owner has taken reasonable measures to keep such information secret and the information derives independent economic value, actual or potential, from not being generally known to and not being ascertainable through proper means by the public," was now considered a federal criminal offense.

It allows the government to prosecute the theft whether it takes place in the United States, on the Internet, or in any international location. The act provides for prison sentences of up to fifteen years and fines up to $500,000.

LIMITATIONS OF THE ACT

While the legislation was conceived and enacted with the best of intentions and while it shows increased awareness of the foreign threat to U.S. businesses, it has so far proved to be largely ineffective and unenforceable. Even former attorney general Janet Reno, a staunch supporter of the need for legislation, has discussed the deficiencies of the law. She has stated publicly that, as a result of the vagaries of the act, she had no intention of aggressively prosecuting potential offenders. During the first five years of the act, every EEA prosecution had to be approved by her, and thus far the U.S. Justice Department has remained extremely selective in choosing cases.

There are many problems with the act. First of all, it will not eliminate true espionage by foreign governments. Espionage has always been illegal, but that has not deterred foreign services from targeting the United States and others for their secrets. And since the economic angle has become more important in recent years, many foreign governments and large corporations are putting more resources toward collecting economic and technical information. A government can save millions of dollars and years of research if it can obtain information already gathered by others rather than having to develop it independently. Most foreign governments are willing to help "their own" gain a competitive edge. Countries use every method previously used against "government targets," including electronic eavesdropping, penetrating computer systems, surveillance, trespassing, blackmail, bribery, planting "moles," and hiring away employees.

Furthermore, it can be difficult to prove that a crime has been committed. The best espionage operations, cloaked in secrecy, are never discovered. If a company can recruit a spy to copy a file and return it unaltered, for example, the company may never know that the information was accessed illegally and passed to a foreign government or company. Companies often assume that the identical technology or proprietary information was simultaneously developed by the foreign company and that it was merely a case of bad luck when, in fact, it was espionage that acquired the information. Intelligence officers and investigators simply don't believe in coincidence.

Another major problem with foreign, government-sponsored espionage, regardless of whether it is economic, political, military, or whatever, is that the offenders are often protected from arrest by diplomatic immunity. So, even if their operations are discovered, the most that can be done is to expel the crook and register a diplomatic complaint with the offending foreign government.

PUNISHING THE OFFENDERS

These limitations are reflected in the arrests made under the act so far. Although the FBI is reportedly investigating more than 800 separate cases under the EEA, only eighteen people have been charged as of this writing. And all of the cases appear to be examples of exceptionally blatant attempts at economic espionage. Four of them involve foreign industrial espionage (South Korea, Taiwan, and China) and the rest are domestic cases. Three of the cases involved FBI sting operations, which may be indicative of a more aggressive approach to countering industrial espionage but which more likely is only the result of a tip being given to the FBI and the ease of running a sting operation with a cooperative potential victim.

The bottom line is that, at least in the near term, the act will not provide significant protection for U.S. businesses. Foreign governments will continue to target U.S. technology, and their approaches probably will get even more sophisticated as the United States raises the bar of deterrence. Company-to-company theft will continue, because as we know very well by now, it is cheaper to steal cutting-edge technology than to develop it.

Couple this with the difficulty in proving that these kinds of crimes have been committed, or who precisely is behind the espionage, and the onus falls back on individual companies to protect themselves from these kinds of attacks.

WHAT CAN BE DONE?

It is imperative that companies with secrets to protect improve their internal security procedures—access control, briefing employees, compartmentalization of information, and so forth—and that they know their employees and the people with whom they do business. Conducting comprehensive due diligence and background investigations on all individuals and the companies they plan to work with, particularly in the international arena, should be standard operating procedure—SOP—for every serious company.

Remember the words of Sun Tzu: "Know your enemy and know yourself." Although the EEA has been used rather sparingly to date, more arrests and convictions will follow as corporate America wakes up to the threat and law enforcement agencies learn more about the modus operandi of states and companies that routinely engage in industrial and economic espionage.

9

ECONOMIC ESPIONAGE, CHINESE STYLE

When the story broke a few years ago about an ethnic Chinese computer scientist employed by the Los Alamos National Laboratory being suspected of having passed highly classified information on nuclear warhead technology to the Chinese government, I was among those intelligence officers who were not in the least surprised. Wen Ho Lee, it appeared, may have been quietly working for China for ten years while enjoying the benefits of U.S. citizenship, life in sunny New Mexico, and a top secret security clearance within one of the Department of Energy's (DOE's) most sensitive research areas. What a surprise!

Whether the Wen Ho Lee story is one of espionage or simple mishandling of classified information, it is representative of the Chinese modus operandi in running foreign intelligence operations. And the case is neither isolated nor unusual. It is indicative of the Chinese government's broad strategy for obtaining technology from the United States and other countries to bolster its competitive position in the global marketplace—militarily and otherwise. The strategy consists of establishing and strengthening information networks, building cooperation with international firms to facilitate technology transfer, and using Chinese nationals to transfer and disseminate technology by studying and working overseas.

And the Chinese are not even quiet about their intentions. During his historic visit to the United States in 1979, Chinese leader Deng Xiaoping boldly shook his finger at the entire Carter cabinet and announced: "We want your most up-to-date technology. Not just that of the early 70s, but the very latest. Do you understand?"

Deng's statement signaled a massive Chinese intelligence initiative to acquire high-tech information, including that most highly guarded technology of all—nuclear—from the United States and its Western allies. The fact that the DOE's weapons labs were on the top of China's target list came as no surprise to anyone in the U.S. intelligence community.

Although Chinese intelligence had been actively targeting Western technology through the use of overseas Chinese since Mao Zedong formed the Peoples' Republic of China after World War II, the effort really started to pick up under Deng Xiaoping's leadership. He announced to the Chinese population, "It doesn't matter if the cat is black or white, as long as it catches mice," and aggressively attempted to push China, using any means at his disposal, into direct head-to-head competition with the West, both militarily and economically.

The first major example of the Chinese push to acquire U.S. secrets occurred in 1986 with the arrest and conviction of Larry Wu-tai Chin, sending shock waves through the CIA and the rest of the U.S. intelligence community. Mr. Chin had been a longtime CIA translator who was found to have been secretly reporting to Chinese intelligence for more than thirty years. That same year it was learned that the Chinese had illegally purchased U.S. defense technology that had been transferred to Israel for the development of Israel's Lavi fighter-bomber. The classified information allowed the Chinese to develop their J-10 fighter-bomber, which was based on the American F-16 Fighting Falcon.

Then, in 1993, another overseas Chinese, philosophy professor Bin Wu, was sentenced to ten years in federal prison for attempting to transfer classified night-vision technology to China. Mr. Wu had been sent to the United States by China's Ministry of State Security (MSS) with orders to become a successful businessman and to steal weapons-related technology. He had established a front company in Hong Kong for the purpose of secretly transferring the technology to China.

In 1994 the U.S. Commerce Department approved the export of machine tools to China over the strong objections of the U.S. military and intelligence officials. It was later learned that some of the sophisticated equipment was shipped to a Chinese defense company that used this equipment to produce parts for fighter aircraft and cruise missiles. Not surprisingly, this occurred while John Huang, a central figure in the "Chinagate" campaign fund-raising controversy, served as a deputy assistant U.S. commerce secretary. Meanwhile, Arkansas restaurant owner Charlie Trie was arranging for Wang Jun, a known Chinese arms dealer with links to the Chinese military, to meet with White House officials. Mr. Huang also brokered a $1 billion deal between his former employer, Indonesia's Lippo Group, and a U.S. firm, Entergy Corp., to build a nuclear power plant in China. The construction of the plant was overseen by the same agency that develops China's nuclear weapons.

By 1994 the problem of safeguarding Chinese and Russian nuclear materials and nuclear tech theft became so great that it prompted President Clinton to announce: "The proliferation of nuclear, biological, and chemical weapons and of the means to deliver them constitutes an extraordinary threat to the national security, foreign policy, and economy of the U.S." He declared the problem a "national emergency."

But in a strange twist of logic, because it was felt to be good for nonproliferation, the United States accelerated its program to provide China and Russia with advanced computers, sensors, and other technology designed to safeguard their nukes. Along with this technology transfer, exchanges between nuclear scientists and labs were encouraged. Predictably, not all of these exchanges concerned only nuclear safeguards and nonproliferation, and the computers and other advanced technology that the United States provided were put to use for other things as well.

In 1994 Los Alamos head Sig Hecker led a delegation of his scientists to the Chinese Academy of Engineering Physics, signaling a renaissance in nuclear cooperation between the United States and China. This visit was followed by return visits by the Chinese to the United States and further technology exchanges in subsequent years. A laissez faire atmosphere prevailed and security at the national labs suffered.

It was 1996, fully twelve years after Wen Ho Lee first allegedly began transferring the "legacy codes" from the secure Los Alamos computer, when the FBI began its investigation into his activities. A year later, Peter Lee (no relation to Wen Ho Lee), a Chinese-born research physicist employed at the Lawrence Livermore Laboratories, admitted to providing classified information on laser and radar technology to China during visits in 1985 and 1997.

These two events sparked U.S. counterintelligence experts into action, and a twenty-five-page report was sent to the White House warning that China poses an "acute intelligence threat" to the U.S. nuclear weapons laboratories and that computers at the labs were constantly being penetrated by unauthorized outsiders.

LAX SECURITY

DOE statistics showed that about 50 percent of the PhDs working at the labs were foreign nationals. Although they were all supposed to be assigned to unclassified areas, they were permitted to socialize freely with individuals working on sensitive projects and were sometimes allowed to visit secure areas under escort. The number of foreign visitors to the labs increased dramatically, and between 1994 and 1996, only 16 percent of the almost 6,000 "criteria country" visitors (including almost 1,500 Chinese) received background investigations. In sum, security was atrocious.

In addition to the poor security, most DOE scientists possessed an arrogant, libertarian attitude toward anything that might in any way impinge on their rights or curtail their activities. Despite the responsibility that went with their top secret security clearances, they resisted efforts to get them to report their foreign travel and their contacts with foreigners and to stop discussing classified information with other, noncleared colleagues. They felt that the cold war was over and saw no need for security and counterintelligence vigilance.

To make matters worse, in an after-action report, the Justice Department concluded that the FBI should have moved against Wen Ho Lee and others much sooner. It stated that the investigators did not need a court order to search Lee's computer, because he had signed a privacy waiver that granted them permission to conduct such a search. The report added, with 20/20 hindsight, that if Lee's computer had been searched back in 1997 without a warrant, the downloads would have been discovered and evidence to convict him would have been obtained. The review also concluded that attorneys at the Justice Department improperly applied a law governing the granting of secret warrants to conduct electronic surveillance by demanding too much evidence instead of determining that sufficient probable cause existed.

This was the operational environment that faced the Chinese intelligence services from the mid-1990s; they recognized the weaknesses in the system and most definitely took advantage of the opportunities presented.

THE CHINESE APPROACH

Here's how it works.

The MSS is the main arm of the Chinese government that governs intelligence collection activities targeted against foreign governments and corporations. It uses a network of recruited agents and informants to collect intelligence abroad. MSS case officers assigned to Chinese embassies and consulates or other quasi-official installations abroad (the New China News Agency, the Civil Aviation Administration of China, and so forth) run the agent/informant networks with guidance from MSS headquarters in Beijing. The agents and informants are, for the most part, ethnic Chinese residents of the target country: overseas Chinese. People just like Mr. Wen Ho Lee.

China is a tightly controlled police state. Virtually all Chinese citizens who work or study abroad, and overseas Chinese who visit their families in China, are routinely contacted and monitored by the MSS. They are asked to keep their eyes and ears open and to report any information they may stumble across. Those who successfully develop access to information of value become candidates for full recruitment by Chinese intelligence. They are given guidance on intelligence requirements and collection techniques, provided with communication plans, and put into direct clandestine contact with MSS case officers or principal agents within the target country. This is SOP—standard operating procedure—for the MSS. The screening process is thorough and effective, and there is no shortage of overseas Chinese intelligence agent candidates who retain some degree of loyalty to their motherland.

Furthermore, cooperation is often not a matter of choice; coercion and threats (usually against family members residing in China) are used, as well as positive incentives (money, privileges, and so forth), to ensure cooperation.

The MSS obtains a huge amount of intelligence information from Chinese students, businessmen, tourists, and officials who visit the United States and other Western countries. Likewise, they are experts at elicitation, especially from innocent overseas Chinese and Western businessmen, scientists, engineers, and other technicians. Those who visit China are wined, dined, and cultivated. Important overseas Chinese are invited to visit China, often Hong Kong, where they are assessed, developed, and often recruited.

The MSS has also taken a few pages out of the French security service's book and frequently bugs visitors' hotel rooms, rifles through briefcases, and copies data from laptops left in hotel rooms and offices. One egregious example of this occurred in 1993 when visiting Deputy Assistant Secretary of Defense Mitchell Wallerstein left his briefcase, filled with highly classified reports, in his Beijing hotel room. This security lapse gave the MSS access to a treasure trove of U.S. defense secrets directly relating to China.

It is understood in Beijing that great powers have neither friends nor enemies, only interests. So much the better for them and the worse for the rest of us.

ECONOMIC ESPIONAGE

A recent incident of economic espionage by China has a similar theme. Huang Dao Pei, a naturalized U.S. citizen, attempted to buy the formula for a hepatitis C diagnostic kit from a fellow scientist at Roche Diagnostics. Roche spent millions of dollars and several years on the development of the product, and China almost obtained the formula for peanuts. We do not yet know the full extent of Huang's betrayal to Roche and his adopted country during the years he worked at Roche, but we can estimate what the cost would have been if he had been successful in stealing the formula for the testing kit. The only reason he was caught was because the fellow scientist turned him in.

Although the FBI won't say, the incident involving Huang Dao Pei was almost certainly part of a well-orchestrated MSS operation. Huang had worked for Roche from 1992 to 1995. During that time, he probably provided a steady stream of proprietary information to his MSS handlers in the United States and China. Then, when he lost his job and consequently his direct access to information of value to China, his MSS case officer directed him to enlist the aid of a friendly scientist working on the hepatitis C project. Unfortunately for Mr. Huang, however, the scientist reported the approach to the FBI. The rest is history.

Huang Dao Pei was the fifth person to be tried under the Economic Espionage Act of 1996. The four who preceded him included two Americans caught spying for competing U.S. firms, and two ethnic Chinese from Taiwan. In one of the Taiwanese cases, $400,000 was offered for proprietary pharmaceutical information. In the other, federal authorities estimate that Taiwan was attempting to steal information that had cost $50 million to develop; the Taiwanese had paid an informant $150,000 to obtain the secret information. Friends and foes alike engage in similar forms of economic espionage.

Again, it's always cheaper to steal a product than to do the research and development from scratch. China (and Taiwan) knows this very well, and it underscores the threat China poses to the U.S. economy through its theft of trade secrets. These are not isolated incidents. The threat is real and growing. As we mentioned in the first chapter, the White House estimates that more than $100 billion is lost to the U.S. economy every year through similar acts of corporate espionage.

Paul Redmond, former counterintelligence chief for the CIA, has described the Chinese Los Alamos espionage case alone as a bigger disaster to the United States than the Soviet atomic spy cases of the 1940s.

Private industry, like government, has a responsibility to take whatever security measures are necessary to guard its proprietary secrets. When they lose, we all lose.

THE "SENSITIVITY" OBSTACLE

An important part of the screening process for a U.S. government security clearance is an evaluation of possible divided loyalties. All naturalized U.S. citizens, not just Chinese, come under intense scrutiny on the loyalty issue. Then, if they are eventually given a clearance despite having close ties to another country, their contacts with former countrymen and relatives are supposed to be routinely monitored for as long as their security clearances remain valid. This is particularly important when the home country involved is known to attempt to suborn its former citizens aggressively and routinely.

Wen Ho Lee was clearly not sufficiently monitored by government security officers after receiving his clearance, nor did Roche keep a close enough eye on Huang Dao Pei. Both the government and Roche must bear the responsibility for this negligence. They should have known better. They should have been aware that these employees were inherently vulnerable, and that they would probably be actively targeted by China's MSS.

Although the loyalty issue is a sensitive one, it must be confronted directly and dispassionately, particularly when national security is at stake. U.S. citizens who have immigrated to our shores are not second-class citizens and should in no way be treated as such. Most of us are the offspring of immigrants. But it must be remembered that as a group they are vulnerable to pressure from their former countries, and when that former country chooses to exploit these individuals as a matter of state policy, we have a real problem on our hands.

10

ECONOMIC ESPIONAGE AND PROTECTION OF INTELLECTUAL PROPERTY

As we said earlier, the main difference between "business intelligence" and "corporate or industrial espionage" is one of legality. Likewise, the difference between "economic intelligence" and "economic espionage" is also one of legality. Collectors of business or economic intelligence use legal methods to gather information on a target, while industrial or economic espionage implies illegal methods such as wiretapping and stealing confidential documents. Japan, for example, is an aggressive collector of economic intelligence, but for the most part it relies on legal methods to gather its information. Other countries, some that might surprise you, often resort to illegal methods to collect their information. This is economic espionage.

Generally, then, when we talk about corporate or industrial espionage, it means one company stealing information from another company, usually within the same country, but not necessarily. The term "economic espionage" is usually reserved for countries that steal secrets from other countries or from companies within other countries. This type of espionage is sanctioned and usually is aided by the government of the country doing the stealing, making it all the more ominous. Government-backed spying on business is not a new thing, but it has been growing exponentially since the end of the cold war.

According to a survey conducted by the American Society for Industrial Security (ASIS), in 1997 alone U.S.-based companies lost an estimated $300 billion in intellectual property to foreign spies. The FBI's estimate for the same year was $435 billion, but that figure included both foreign and domestic espionage. (Both of these figures far exceed the $100 billion figure estimated by the White House, but whatever figure you care to believe, the losses are clearly huge.) In the same year, the FBI documented more than 1,100 incidents of economic espionage and 550 suspected incidents. More than 700 foreign counterintelligence investigations involving economic espionage are currently pending before the bureau. The incidents included the theft of customer lists, chemical formulas, and other proprietary information by some of our closest allies, including the United Kingdom, Japan, Israel, and France. The FBI survey disclosed that high-tech companies were the most frequent targets of foreign spies, followed by manufacturing and service industries. The spies targeted research and development strategies, manufacturing and marketing plans, and customer lists.

Despite these losses, ASIS estimates that only 63 percent of Fortune 1000 companies have formal safeguard programs in place to thwart economic espionage.

The CIA has identified the governments of France, Israel, China, and Russia as among a handful of nations that are "extensively engaged in economic espionage" against the United States. It also confirmed that Japan, an ally viewed by many as among the most unscrupulous in trying to steal U.S. technology, engages in "mostly legal" collection efforts. The CIA report, which went to the Senate Select Committee on Intelligence, added: "We have only identified about a half-dozen governments that we believe have extensively engaged in economic espionage as we define it."

The Clinton administration was so concerned about the increased threat of economic espionage that it formed the National Counterintelligence Center (NACIC) in 1994 to pool the resources of the FBI, CIA, DIA, NSA, and the State Department to combat economic espionage.

Some of the intrusive methods the NACIC has found to be used by foreign countries include:

- eavesdropping by wiretapping, bugging offices, or capturing cellular telephone conversations;
- penetrating computer networks;

- stealing proprietary information contained in drawings and documents and on floppy disks and CD ROMs;
- using the services of prostitutes for blackmail purposes;
- using a "swallow" (an attractive woman) or a "raven" (a handsome man) to form a close personal relationship with an employee with access to trade secrets;
- hiring a competitor's employee who has valuable knowledge;
- bribing a company's supplier or employee;
- planting an agent or "mole" in a company with the mission to compromise key employees, tap into computer databases, and intercept communications to ferret out confidential information, technologies, and other information.

Essentially, all the techniques used by trained intelligence operations officers are used by foreign governments to conduct economic espionage. Bribes, breaking and entering, and the use of exchange students and visiting professors can all be added to the list of intrusive and illegal methods used. It's a no-holds-barred activity. Some countries, France, for example, will stop at nothing to obtain economic secrets. Remember the story about how France had installed bugs in the first-class seats of its Air France planes that flew between New York and Paris? I wonder just how many confidential conversations between U.S. industry leaders, seated side by side, engaged in putting the final touches on their sensitive negotiating positions, were recorded in the Concorde as it flew high above the ocean. The information obtained in this activity alone must have given the French an enormous advantage over U.S. and other competing firms.

It appears that the fact that France is a close ally of the United States makes no difference whatsoever; economic espionage is a matter of national policy for France, as it is for a number of other "allies" as well. We discussed China's economic espionage activities in the United States at length in a previous chapter. I guess China would not be considered a close ally of the United States, certainly not as close as France. So, perhaps we can more easily excuse China's behavior than France's.

But what about a really close ally—one that has received billions and billions in U.S. foreign aid? Let's examine the conduct of Israel, which has been described as the country that implements the most aggressive program of economic espionage against the United States of any U.S. ally.

ISRAEL VS. UNITED STATES

Israel's espionage against the United States is distinctive because of the close cultural, political, military, and economic ties that exist between the two countries. No other ally is more dependent on the United States for its survival than Israel; no other ally receives more in the form of U.S. security and intelligence assistance, or is more dependent on having close, cooperative ties with the United States. Some would go as far as to suggest that the state of Israel would not exist today were it not for its "special relationship" with the United States.

Israel's economic espionage against the United States really began in earnest back in the 1960s when Israel's defense ministry created what eventually evolved into its Office of Special Tasks (LAKAM). LAKAM's main task was to strengthen Israel's defense ministry through the collection of scientific intelligence primarily through technical and human penetrations of the U.S. defense establishment. Other units of Israel's intelligence community that routinely engage in economic espionage include its foreign intelligence service, Mossad, and a new organization within the defense ministry called the Security Authority (Malmab).

Targets of Israel's economic espionage have included technology for artillery gun tubes, coatings for missile reentry vehicles, avionics, missile telemetry, and aircraft communications systems.

In one case in 1986, three Israeli air force officers were caught while trying to steal 50,000 pages of technical documents relating to aerial surveillance equipment from Recon/Optical, Inc., a U.S. defense contractor. For at least a year before their arrest, the three Israeli officers had been exploiting an official liaison relationship and passing proprietary information from Recon/Optical to a competing Israeli firm, El Op Electro-Optics Industries. An arbitration panel later ordered Israel to pay Recon/Optical $3 million in damages for what it found to be "perfidious" illegal acts. Nevertheless, Recon/Optical was brought to the point of bankruptcy by the thefts. The stolen optics technology apparently provided critical elements of Israel's first durable reconnaissance satellite, the Ofek-3.

Other examples of aggressive Israeli intelligence collection against the U.S. defense establishment included the theft of classified F-16 blueprints out of the General Dynamics plant in Fort Worth, Texas, and an attempt to export U.S. cluster bomb technology. Both of these cases occurred during the early 1980s and resulted in the arrests of the Israeli agents involved. In another case, Israeli agents colluded with a Connecticut company named NAPCO to export sensitive technology for chrome plating the inside of 120 millimeter tank barrels. NAPCO pleaded guilty to violating U.S. export law and was fined $750,000, but no Israelis were prosecuted. In other cases, the Justice Department charged an official of the Science Applications International Corporation with illegally transferring U.S. missile defense technology to Israel through high-ranking Israeli military officers, and Israel was caught improperly transferring U.S. technology for remotely piloted vehicles to the Israeli company Mazlot, which later used the information to underbid its U.S. competitors.

In May 1985 Richard Smyth, an American Jew, was charged with smuggling 810 krytons—electronic triggers for nuclear weapons—to Israel. He was released on $100,000 bail but failed to appear for trial and later turned up living in Israel.

Sometimes Israel doesn't have to resort to the theft of U.S. technical secrets; U.S. representatives simply give it to them "under the table." For example, a 1997 FBI memorandum revealed that David Tenenbaum, a deeply religious Jew and a civilian Department of Defense employee with the U.S. Army Tank Automotive and Armaments Command (TACOM), admitted giving "non-releasable classified information to every Israeli liaison officer assigned to TACOM over the past 10 years." The information passed by Tenenbaum included classified data on theater missile defense systems, the Bradley fighting vehicle, ceramic armor, and other weapons systems. Tenenbaum also appears to have furthered Israel's commercial interests as well, since the Israeli company Elbit now offers upgrades of the U.S. Army's Bradley fighting vehicle, and Israel has attempted to export its U.S. technology–derived Arrow theater missile defense system to Turkey.

FROM THE UNITED STATES TO CHINA, VIA ISRAEL

For those who scoff at Israel's economic espionage activities targeted against the United States and its NATO allies, saying that Israel is, after all, a close ally, and U.S. secrets are safe with that country, there is the problem of technology transfer. In short, Israel steals it (or is given it under military exchange agreements), repackages it, and sells it to our adversaries, including China.

On 19 May 2000 the *Washington Times* cited U.S. intelligence sources as saying that Israel would deliver a high-technology AWACS (Airborne Warning And Control System) platform to China. This is U.S. technology that will significantly enhance China's ability to target enemy forces over the horizon and will result in a huge increase in China's command and control capability. This delivery will be the first of several (three to seven) AWACS systems being produced by Israel specifically for China. The platforms will contain the advanced Israeli Phalcon radar system, derived from the U.S. AWACS model, and will cost about $250 million each.

THE DUAL LOYALTY ISSUE AGAIN

We discussed the issue of dual loyalty in the chapter on Chinese espionage; the same applies for Israel. And as with the Chinese, it is not just a case of divided loyalty; it is a case of the mother country actively pursuing a policy of suborning its overseas residents when it is in the mother country's best interests. Many Jews have a deep loyalty to Israel, and Israeli intelligence routinely attempts to take advantage of this loyalty when it pleases them.

The Jonathan Pollard affair is a prime example of these forces at work. U.S. and Western counterintelligence must accept these facts and deal with them accordingly. The CIA does. During the years I was with the Agency, it refused to send Jewish case officers to posts in Israel for just this reason; the risk of exposing its case officers to Israeli recruitment and elicitation efforts on Israel's home turf was determined to be simply too great.

This is evidenced by the U.S. Defense Investigative Service, which prepared a profile of Israel's economic espionage activities in 1996. After noting Israel's "voracious appetite" for information on U.S. defense technologies, the profile stated that Israel's highly productive collection efforts in the United States were facilitated by "ethnic targeting" and "the strong ethnic ties to Israel present in the U.S."

Virtually no serious official in the U.S. government will deny the reality of ethnic targeting by some foreign intelligence services. They will also agree that Israel, China, Taiwan, and South Korea are the leaders in this regard. Both the FBI and the CIA have long been aware of ethnic targeting and are sensitive to it when investigating cases of the theft of proprietary or classified information. The CIA has stated publicly that Israel's intelligence services "depend heavily on various Jewish communities and organizations abroad for recruiting agents and eliciting informants."

WHAT THE FUTURE HOLDS

Unless peace quickly comes to the Middle East, which is highly unlikely, Israel's efforts to acquire badly needed technology through economic espionage will probably increase. Israel's national priorities are actively promoting an export-oriented technology sector featuring strong software, Internet services, biotechnology firms, and other high-tech industries. But as long as it is forced to spend the bulk of its gross national product on defense, it will be forced to acquire needed technology as cheaply as possible. And as we have learned, it is always cheaper to steal it than to invent it through expensive research and development programs.

Given the pace of technological innovation and obsolescence, the risks associated with investment in new product development increase, which militates for a policy of even more aggressive economic espionage. Look for more joint ventures between Israel's technology-based industries and U.S. organizations; ventures that provide access and opportunity for the theft of technology.

Economic espionage is a fact of life in the world order, but Israel's chutzpah is unique among the nations that engage in it. Few allies are more strategically and economically dependent on the United States, or have conducted a more aggressive policy of economic and foreign espionage against their benefactor.

ECHELON

Even the United States has been accused of government-backed economic spying on its closest allies.

To wit, the European Union (EU) recently alleged that the world's five leading English-speaking nations have engaged in a joint project called "Echelon" to provide advantages to their domestic industries in international competitive bids by intercepting e-mail, faxes, and phone conversations. The EU parliament plans to open a major debate concerning the legality and ethics of the project and of electronic eavesdropping by U.S. intelligence agencies in general.

Among the allegations is that information obtained from intercepted phone calls between Brazilian officials and the French firm Thompson-CSF during 1994 was used by the United States to swing a $1.3 billion radar contract away from Thompson to the U.S. firm Raytheon.

Similarly, a few years earlier, in 1990, there were claims that the NSA had intercepted telephone calls between Indonesian officials and officers with the Japanese satellite manufacturer NEC Corporation regarding a pending $200 million telecommunications deal. The U.S.-owned AT&T Corporation was also a bidder for the contract, but the intercepted conversations indicated that Indonesia would award the contract to NEC.

In both cases, the NSA intelligence intercepts reportedly indicated that illegal bribes to Indonesian and Brazilian officials were influencing the awarding of the contracts to the non-U.S. firms. In the Indonesian case, it took the direct intervention of then U.S. president George Bush to convince the Indonesian president to at least split the contract between NEC and AT&T, which is what eventually happened.

In yet another case, the French intelligence service accused the United States of using its intelligence services to collude with Microsoft Corporation to develop software that would allow the United States to spy on computer users around the globe. The French claimed that NSA helped install secret programs on Microsoft software on 90 percent of its computers in use worldwide. (Note: Based on my experience in the U.S. intelligence community, this accusation is pure hogwash. That is not to say, however, that such a feat would not be possible to achieve in a country with lower ethical and legal standards than the United States.)

In fact, a close reading of all of the cases involving charges of U.S. espionage on its competitors, through the Echelon project and unilaterally, reveals U.S. intelligence detecting foreign firms trying to beat out U.S. firms for third-country business by bribery. In each case, the intelligence was used to level the playing field for the U.S. firm, usually in the form of a State Department démarche to the third country in question.

WHEN EAVESDROPPING IS OKAY

Although U.S. authorities have consistently denied that its SIGINT (signals intelligence) capabilities are put to use to support U.S. private industry, in cases like this where illegal methods such as bribes may have been used to secure bids to the detriment of U.S. firms, it is reasonable to expect that the U.S. government would make exceptions. The corporate playing fields are different in Europe and Asia, for example, than they are in the United States. The American law that bars U.S. corporations from bribing foreign officials, the U.S. Corrupt Foreign Practices Act, is viewed as "quaint" in Europe and Asia, where the payment of bribes to obtain contracts is "business as usual." In fact, for many countries, the payment of bribes is not only legal, but also can be written off as a business tax deduction.

NSA routinely collects signals intelligence from listening posts located all over the globe. These signals include telephone conversations, faxes, and e-mails. However, the volume of the information collected is so great that it would be impossible to transcribe and translate (and sometimes decode) all of it into usable form. Most of it just sits untouched on huge reels of recording tape. It's only when the computers pick up key words or combinations of words (for example, president/assassinate, explosives/embassy), or when individual phone lines are targeted (for example, between Iranian government offices and the United States) that transcriptions of the conversations are automatically ordered. In other cases, it takes a clue that something has taken place or is about to take place to set the computers in search of specific information that may have been collected.

LA BELLE DISCO

This is what happened during the investigation that followed the 5 April 1986 bombing of La Belle Disco, a popular hangout for U.S. military personnel, in what was then West Berlin. At the outset, circumstantial evidence, including a public statement calling for Arab assaults on American interests worldwide made by Libyan leader Colonel Moammar Kadafy two weeks before the attack, strongly pointed toward Libya as being behind the heinous act of terrorism on German soil that killed two U.S. servicemen and a young Turkish woman and injured 229 others. However, hard proof was lacking. That proof came when NSA searched its databanks of intercepted conversations between Kadafy and the Libyan intelligence service and the Libyan embassy in what was then East Berlin during the time frame immediately preceding and following the bombing.

The result was clear and indisputable proof, in the form of recorded telephone conversations, that Kadafy personally authorized the attack and that it was carried out by agents of Libyan intelligence. One of the conversations used as evidence came about three weeks before the attack. It was from the Libyan intelligence headquarters in Tripoli to the embassy in East Berlin calling for an attack "with as many victims as possible." Another came from the embassy to Tripoli a few hours after the attack, saying: "At 1:30 in the morning one of the acts was carried out with success, without leaving a trace behind."

West German police later used telephone intercepts to track down the ringleader of the attack, a Libyan intelligence officer stationed at the East Berlin embassy, who was caught hiding out in Rome.

The result was an announcement by then president Ronald Reagan that the United States had irrefutable proof of Kadafy's guilt in the matter, and that a retaliatory air attack had been carried out on two Libyan cities, including Kadafy's palace and tent, on 14 April 1986. Unfortunately, the U.S. Naval warplanes missed Kadafy, but his adopted child and several other household members were killed in the attack. The attack so frightened Kadafy that he went into a deep, dark depression that lasted until he emerged again a few years later to blast PanAm 103 out of the air over Lockerbie, Scotland.

The fact that the United States routinely monitors communications in Europe and elsewhere for economic bribery activity and other legitimate means such as counterterrorism is appropriate, and not a secret. On the economic bribery issue, former CIA director James Woolsey has confirmed publicly that the practice of gathering intelligence on corrupt practices by companies and governments abroad has long been accepted in Washington: "We have spied on that in the past. I hope . . . that the U.S. government continues to spy on bribery." He added that this type of spying was justified, because European companies had a "national culture" of bribery to obtain international contracts.

CANADIAN ESPIONAGE

Even our friendly neighbor to the north, Canada, is not above economic espionage.

Mike Frost, author of *Spyworld,* a book about his career in Canada's secret service (CSE), said that Canadian spies once eavesdropped on the U.S. ambassador to Canada while he was discussing a pending deal with China on a mobile telephone. According to Mr. Frost, the CSE used that information to undercut efforts by the United States to land a $2.5 billion Chinese grain sale. He went on to say that as far back as 1981, Canada had been using U.S.-produced spy technology, much of which is obtained under strict intelligence liaison agreements between the two countries, to eavesdrop on the U.S. ambassador.

PIRACY AND COUNTERFEITING

Counterfeiting and product rip-offs are growing, nasty industries. Microsoft alone loses hundreds of millions of dollars each year through the illegal manufacture and sale of rip-off copies of its software. For many years, Taiwan, for example, has been a major source of illegal copies of Microsoft and other computer software, perfumes, books, video and audio cassettes, and everything else imaginable all the way to Polo shirts and Levi jeans. It's a particularly nasty business, because it's so easy to obtain an original product to copy—all one has to do is purchase one. And when nations routinely permit counterfeits and knockoffs to be produced and sold openly, prosecution is made very difficult.

The digital nature of software makes it particularly vulnerable to quick and easy duplication and distribution. According to the Business Software Alliance, in 1998 software piracy resulted in losses of nearly $1 billion in U.S. tax revenue, $4.5 billion in wages, and 109,000 jobs in the United States alone. The study didn't even mention the losses to Microsoft and other software manufacturers. And the problem is growing: In 1999 Microsoft reported a total of more than 4.3 million units of counterfeit software seized by law enforcement authorities, nearly five times the amount recovered the previous year. This doesn't even count the software that is distributed and shared freely over the Internet. And the old canard about software rip-offs not being as good quality as the real thing is simply not true; especially now, with digital technology. They are often as crisp and clear as the originals.

Antipiracy liaison between Hong Kong Customs and the Chinese government has been studying ways to stem the flow of pirated CDs across the border from Hong Kong into China. In 1998 Chinese customs officers seized 38.5 million pirated CDs and 68 production lines and arrested 1,610 people involved in the cross-border smuggling activities. The Guangdong provincial government (operating along the same border between Hong Kong and China) seized an additional 33 million pirated CDs, 2.5 million pirated books, and 21 production lines and arrested 1,790 people involved in the illicit trade.

It's an international problem that will take close international cooperation to stop. But that cooperation won't come easily, especially when there is so much money involved in product counterfeiting and piracy, and rogue nations continue to condone, or at least turn a blind eye, to the activity, as you will see from the following example of an operation that sought to shut down the illegal sale of counterfeit Bausch & Lomb products in Ecuador.

COUNTERFEIT RAY BANS

In mid-1994 Bausch & Lomb became aware that cheap knockoffs of its Ray-Ban Wayfarer, Aviator, and other models of sunglasses were appearing in market kiosks near the Hotel Intercontinental in Quito. They wanted to determine if, indeed, counterfeits were being sold, and if so, who was the source of the supply and what was the distribution network. Finally, they wanted to exert influence on the Ecuadorian government at the highest levels to urge the police to confiscate the rip-offs and arrest the criminals behind the activity.

The first step was to send a local investigator to visit the kiosks and shops in the area and to photograph and purchase samples of the counterfeit glasses on display to be used as evidence. Several sale locations were identified and photographed, including such prominent shops as Taty, Scarlett, and Sacos, where the rip-offs were being sold at an average price of $15 per pair. The counterfeits looked like real Bausch & Lomb products, right down to the cases and stickers on the lenses, but a close examination showed vastly inferior workmanship, particularly on the welds on the frames. As they used to say in Vietnam, they were "same, but not same-same."

Then, posing as an importer wanting to bring large quantities of the glasses into Latin America, the investigator learned that the frames and cases were being shipped into Ecuador by sea from Panama and overland from Colombia, and that the lenses were ground and fitted at a location in Guayaquil on the coast. Further investigation and surveillance revealed that there was a warehouse in the market area called Ipiales Martek. The warehouse was owned by one Lenin Martinez, who belonged to a cooperative called Libertad, Paz y Justicia (Liberty, Peace, and Justice), which was known to be involved in black market activities. The investigator subsequently confirmed that Martinez was the largest distributor of counterfeit Ray-Bans in Quito.

Armed with this knowledge, we contacted the U.S. embassy and urged them to make an official démarche to the Ecuadorian government under the U.S. Trademark Counterfeiting Act of 1984. We urged the embassy to pressure the Ecuadorians to raid the kiosks and shops, arrest the individuals involved, confiscate the counterfeit sunglasses, and destroy them. The U.S. embassy's actions were (predictably) not very strong, however, and resulted in the confiscation and destruction of only a few cases of sunglasses and no arrests. The fact that billions of dollars are lost each year to counterfeiters on this ilk, an amount that includes lost product sales, jobs, and policing costs, is somehow lost on a government with larger problems (narcotics, terrorism, and so forth) on its mind. The burden for counterintelligence activities of this sort must therefore rest with the companies that are being hurt.

DEFENDING YOUR COMPANY

The first step toward keeping a company's secrets from going out the door is to identify what it is that competitors would want and then to put in place reasonable levels of security to protect it. Any company that does not have some sort of information protection policy in place deserves to lose its secrets.

Physical security (locks, alarms, safes, fences, intrusion detection systems, and so forth) is important; procedures for the secure handling and storage of sensitive material should be implemented. An information security plan should be implemented to protect computers and computer files, and above all, procedures must be implemented for the secure destruction of classified information—the office shredder could be a company's best investment.

But these safeguards will not prevent a disgruntled or venal employee from using her access to strip a company of its proprietary secrets, and this is where the real problem lies. Preemployment background checks on every employee with access to sensitive information are an absolute must, as are due diligence investigations of every joint venture partner, particularly foreign partners, with whom sensitive technology may be shared.

Visiting scientists, technicians, and students, particularly those from foreign countries that have a reputation for using their citizens to collect information for the mother countries (China, Japan, Taiwan, South Korea, and Israel, to name a few), should be checked out thoroughly and strictly denied access to proprietary information.

Boeing Corporation reportedly prohibits its employees from sending sensitive data by fax from Asia and Europe. Hewlett-Packard warns its employees not to leave laptop computers containing sensitive information unattended in hotel rooms. The French company Aerospatiale requires that officers involved in sensitive negotiations return to France to discuss strategy rather than trusting phone lines to exchange sensitive information. Northern Telecom, the Canadian telecommunications giant, does the same.

Some of these practices may appear extreme, but in every case where security is concerned, the countermeasures taken should reflect the degree of the threat and the sensitivity of the information to be protected. There would certainly have to be a lot at stake for a company to fly its negotiators back to its home turf rather than to trust the international phone lines, but sometimes these kinds of security measures may be totally appropriate.

11

SOURCE PROTECTION

Perhaps the most recurring dilemma in the intelligence profession is source protection. By its very nature, intelligence is confidential information obtained from confidential sources. When the sources of the confidential information are compromised, information from those sources dries up rapidly.

The debate over the use of intelligence is a daily struggle between the intelligence community and its customers. Simply put, if the use of the intelligence will blow the source, intelligence officers will fight against using the information. But the customers argue that the intelligence is worthless if it can't be used. And the battle is joined.

For instance, if the CIA learns from a sensitive penetration of a drug cartel that a large shipment of cocaine will enter Miami on a specific ship on a specific date, the DEA will want to be there to intercept the shipment before the cocaine reaches the streets. As a law enforcement agency, it will also want to bust the smugglers (one of whom is our source). That's their job. But what if the drug bust would result in the source being blown (as it would in this case)? It is the CIA's job to protect its sources and methods. If the source's information is acted upon and the bust is made, that would put the source in extreme jeopardy. The CIA could not let this happen.

As soon as the shipment is intercepted by the DEA, the cartel's leaders would start looking for the leak that caused the drug bust. Since this kind of information would be very closely held, on a "need to know" basis within the ranks of the cartel, only a few individuals would have had access to it. Therefore, it wouldn't take long before the finger would be pointed at a very small number of people who had access to the information, including the CIA's source.

In a case like this, it would be so likely that the smugglers would eventually learn the identity of the source that it would be too risky to leave the source in place. The source would therefore have to be jerked out of the cold and placed in protective custody even before the bust could take place. The factors that would be weighed by the two sides in the decision to make the bust or not would be the value of the source versus the value of the shipment.

ROCKETS OVER TAIWAN

The desire to act on intelligence when there is a clear advantage in doing so is so strong that nameless, faceless intelligence sources often fall victim to political expediency. Take the 1996 case of the Chinese missiles that were fired in the direction of Taiwan. In an effort to assuage the ire of the population that considered the incident to be tantamount to an act of war, the Taiwan defense ministry issued a statement to reassure its citizens that the threat was really a minor one. It declared that the missiles were unarmed and only contained devices to record their accuracy. That statement alone was sufficient to tip off the Communist Chinese security services that somebody very high up in their own government or military might be spying for Taiwan. The information concerning the nature of the warheads (or lack thereof) and the electronics on the missiles was highly classified and was only available to a select few officials who had a "need to know" the information.

The resulting MSS counterintelligence investigation lasted three years and resulted in the arrest, conviction for spying, and execution of Major General Liu Lian-kun, General Liu's mistress (implicated as a courier and "bag woman"), and Senior Colonel Shao Zeng-shong (an accomplice). The loss of General Liu and his assistants to Taiwan's espionage network in China was inestimable.

Here are the events that led to the blunder. Three Chinese M9 missiles were launched by China on 16 March 1996, two weeks before the Taiwanese presidential elections. They landed thirty-five miles off the coast of Taiwan's largest port, Kaohsiung, in the south, and twenty-three miles from Keelung, the country's second largest port, in the north. During the missile exercises, General Liu had clandestinely informed Taipei that the missiles contained dummy warheads, along with additional information concerning their configuration and Chinese troop deployments and strengths at the time.

The announcement concerning the benign nature of the missiles was made by the Taiwanese government in an effort to discourage voters from supporting a call for a unilateral declaration of independence. It was a purely political decision that overruled the objections of Taiwan's intelligence community. However, realizing that the release of this sensitive information would place General Liu in extreme jeopardy, authorization was given to exfiltrate him out of China and to bring him to the safety of Taiwan. But glitches occurred when bureaucratic snafus in Taiwan, combined with rather swift Communist Chinese counterintelligence action, resulted in delays in actually implementing the plan. Soon the window of opportunity for a secure exfiltration of the agent was lost forever, and an immensely valuable source was sacrificed.

When the whole story finally came out, it was learned that General Liu had been recruited by Taiwan in the early 1990s when he was representing a Peoples' Liberation Army (PLA) front company in Hong Kong. Liu's motivation for accepting recruitment was classic. He had been (wrongly) implicated in an army corruption scandal and had been denied a (well-deserved) promotion. So he decided to right the wrong by getting even with his PLA bosses.

In addition to exacting revenge for his mistreatment, General Liu appears to have been very well paid by Taiwan for his services. Chinese investigators were said to have found almost $2 million stashed in Liu's home and deposited in overseas bank accounts. Again, this appears to have been a classic recruitment operation, with revenge as the stated motive that provided the rationalization for General Liu's actions, and money that provided the real basis for his continuing espionage.

But it all didn't just end here. When the Chinese MSS started probing into this affair, the net for the search of Taiwan's agents spread well beyond General Liu and his pair of accomplices. The counterintelligence probe uncovered a number of other Taiwan agents, including the deputy chief of Hainan Province, Lin Ke-cheng, who was sentenced to life in prison in August 1999. Lin and nine of his colleagues were convicted of providing economic, political, and other kinds of information to Taiwan. Then, in October 1999, Wang

Ping, a local official in Nanchong, Sichuan Province, was sentenced to ten years in prison for working as an agent for Taiwan's military intelligence arm.

Also as a result of the probe, hundreds of PLA officers and all of its defense attachés and diplomats who deal with security matters have been required to provide information on their foreign bank accounts and financial holdings.

In short, the Taiwan defense department's politically motivated statement not only led to the loss of an important intelligence asset, but it also wreaked havoc on Taiwan's entire network of spies on the mainland and lowered its capability to produce reliable intelligence on the Chinese threat for years to come.

WHEN SOURCES DO DUMB THINGS

Although protecting sources is the responsibility of the case officer, agents often can't be protected from some of the dumb breaches of security they themselves commit when they become complacent and cocky, or when something unforeseen happens. For this reason, it is important to build security firewalls, or cutouts, into the operation. They are placed between the agent and his or her handlers to limit the damage of exposure and to prevent the entire operation from becoming unraveled from the bottom up.

Following is a story of a case I handled in Hong Kong that illustrates how precautionary measures that are built into an operation from the start can prevent catastrophic damage to an intelligence-gathering network.

THE PORTCALLER

Portcaller operations have always been a staple of CIA activity abroad. CIA headquarters instructed stations located in port cities around the globe to participate in the program. This was particularly true during the cold war era.

The idea was to recruit seamen working on ships that call regularly on Chinese, North Korean, Vietnamese, and Soviet ports. Once recruited, the seamen agents would be tasked to take panoramic pictures of the harbors and the ships in each of the ports they visited and to jot down the names of the other ships and the dates of their visits, type of cargo loaded and unloaded, and so forth.

If photography was not possible because of security restrictions (which was often the case in Communist ports), the written reporting (names of ships, and so forth) would be all that would be required. This portcaller information was important to intelligence analysts who were charged with the responsibility of tracking shipping in and out of Communist ports. The information from the portcallers would be checked against, and collated with, information from satellites that routinely photographed the target ports. (The problem with the satellite reporting was that cloud cover often obscured the ports for days or weeks at a time, particularly during the rainy season, and the photos often did not reveal the names of the ships in port because of resolution problems or the high angles of the shots. Taken together, however, the satellite and portcaller information provided some pretty thorough coverage of the target ports.)

All Hong Kong–based case officers were familiar with the portcaller program, and most were deeply involved in at least the spotting aspects of it. They all contributed to it in one degree or another. Most of us, for example, were quite familiar with the usual watering places of visiting seamen and would stop by on nights we were out on the town to troll for prospective agent candidates. Hong Kong had a number of bars that catered to seamen, the most famous of which was the Three Sisters Bar in Kowloon.

SPOTTING AT THE THREE SISTERS BAR

The Three Sisters was a small, friendly place (actually run by three sisters) that was home to many a visiting sailor. The seamen would sometimes run up large bills that they were unable to pay when it came time for them to leave Hong Kong. The sisters would simply have them sign a tab and stuff it in a large brandy snifter behind the bar. When the sailor returned, sometimes months or even years later, he would remind one of the sisters of his bill, and she would dig it out of the overfilled snifter for him to pay off before proceeding to run up another bill. Ships of all nationalities that passed in the night while bound for Hong Kong would often flash signals back and forth saying: "See you at the Three Sisters."

The Hong Kong Seamen's Club was another favorite fishing hole for the CIA case officers and their principal agents. In some ways, it was better than bars like the Three Sisters, because many of the sailors off of Communist ships couldn't afford even the cheap beer sold in Kowloon bars, and the club was an inexpensive place for seamen to while away their time and hang out while their ships were in port.

The Communist seamen were, of course, much tougher recruitment targets than non-Communist sailors. This was primarily the result of the security training they were given before they left their countries, the ever-watchful security officers assigned to keep tabs on them while they were at sea and in port, and their general lack of sophistication and ability to speak foreign languages. But their value as portcaller agents was usually much greater because of the better and more frequent access to the target ports they enjoyed.

It was at the Hong Kong Seamen's Club that a principal agent I was handling—his (fictional) digraph was TTSEEK (pronounced T T seek)—spotted a young mainland Chinese sailor who was assigned as a radio operator on a Chinese cargo ship. Let's call him TTSPARKS.

TTSPARKS

TTSPARKS was the perfect portcaller agent candidate. He was an ethnic Chinese working on a Communist Chinese ship that called regularly on ports in China, North Korea, and Vietnam. He also had a responsible job that afforded him privacy to do his photography (the radio room had its own porthole from which he could take his clandestine photos of the harbor and the other ships) and to write his reports (he was often alone in the radio room). The fact that he was a radio operator was an added plus, because it opened up a wide range of clandestine agent communication possibilities down the road.

TTSEEK was a Hong Kong Chinese originally from Fukien Province in China. He was a longtime principal agent whose main task was to spot for new agent talent among the Communist Chinese community in Hong Kong. I was his handler at the time.

TTSEEK spotted TTSPARKS sitting alone drinking a Coke in the atrium at the local seamen's club in Hong Kong. TTSEEK knew TTSPARKS was from one of the Chinese ships presently moored in the harbor from a conversation he had overheard between TTSPARKS and some of the other Chinese seamen earlier in the day. Those conversations were in the Fukinese dialect, a language TTSEEK spoke fluently, and he used this to his advantage to open a conversation with the prospective agent. With the ice broken and rapport building between the two Fukinese, TTSEEK offered to buy TTSPARKS a beer. That beer led to several more and rapport grew and grew, and TTSPARKS revealed that he was a communications officer aboard one of the Chinese freighters in the harbor. Then there was dinner at a local Fukinese restaurant with more beers and more rapport, until the night ended with

TTSEEK escorting TTSPARKS back to his ship. The pair agreed to meet the following day for lunch, but at a location away from the seaman's club, thereby injecting the first bit of the clandestine into the operation.

TTSEEK signaled for an emergency meeting, and we met at our regular safehouse the following morning. He recounted the events of the day before and described TTSPARKS and his ship. We agreed that TTSEEK had found a live one with excellent access and strong potential as a portcaller asset, and discussed how to proceed with the development in the short time available— TTSPARKS's ship was scheduled to leave for Canton in two days. TTSEEK had used an alias with TTSPARKS (standard CIA tradecraft for these kinds of operations), and we decided to use a "false flag" commercial approach to give us further protection from discovery in case of a flap. TTSEEK and I had used this cover several times before, so we were both familiar with the drill.

During his lunch meeting with TTSPARKS, TTSEEK eased into his pitch. Playing on what we perceived to be TTSPARKS's susceptibilities (money and lack of advancement and recognition in his job), TTSEEK explained that he worked for a French commercial research firm that was interested in looking into investment possibilities in China, North Korea, and Vietnam. As part of this research, he needed people like TTSPARKS to provide accurate information concerning what types of cargo were really going in and out of selected ports. TTSEEK explained that although there were statistics for most of this type of information, Communist countries often inflated these figures to provide a brighter picture for potential investors and trading partners. (TTSPARKS bought this latter statement because he knew it to be absolutely true.) TTSEEK said that the research firm just needed some way to spot-check the information that was being fed to outside investors and trading partners. He added that the company was willing to pay its researchers well for the information, as long as the collection process was kept confidential so as not to affect the accuracy of the information being reported.

TTSPARKS was offered a salary of approximately $300 a month (about four times what he was earning on the ship) to be deposited for him in a Hong Kong bank. In addition, he would be given a $500 recruitment bonus in cash. TTSEEK explained that all he had to do to earn this money was to take photos of the ships in the harbor from his commo shack porthole and keep notes on the names of the ships and possibly their cargoes and the dates of their port visits. Then, each time a ship called at Hong Kong, he would meet with TTSEEK to turn over film and notes and be debriefed on what he saw and heard.

If he agreed in principle with this, TTSEEK would introduce him to his French boss to finalize the arrangements and to provide him with a camera, film, and further instructions on how to carry out his new duties. TTSPARKS agreed, and a meeting was set for the following evening at an out-of-the-way restaurant.

The following evening was a great success. I was introduced as François du Bois, director of research for a fictitious firm with a long, complicated French name. I wore a light disguise, consisting of a mustache, heavy French glasses, and a slicked-back hairstyle. To further enhance the cover story, TTSEEK (who was a true polyglot) and I spoke only French together during the evening. TTSEEK translated the French into Fukinese for TTSPARKS.

The recruitment meeting couldn't have gone better. TTSPARKS bought the cover story and was delighted with the opportunity to earn extra money. I had him sign a confidentiality agreement to strengthen the concept of security in his mind, gave him an idiot-proof 35-millimeter camera and several rolls of film, and briefed him on his duties. In addition to the photography and notes on shipping in each harbor, I also asked him to keep his ears open for any information, economic or political, that might affect foreign investment. This last requirement was a long shot, but TTSPARKS had mentioned that he attended regular political meetings with other members of the officer staff on board ship and occasionally in Chinese ports, so I decided to throw it out as well. One never knows, I thought.

It was a huge mistake.

COLLECTION IN CANTON

When TTSPARKS's ship arrived in the port of Canton, he immediately went about the task of photographing and noting the names of all the ships in the harbor at the time. In two days he had taken a full roll of thirty-six exposures from his porthole, giving a panoramic view of the harbor as his ship slowly turned on the axis of its anchor. His notes on ship names, nationalities, and cargoes were copious, and all of this information was hidden in a carefully selected hiding place in the radio shack. Things were going very well indeed up to this point.

Then, on the third day in the port of Canton, a meeting was called by the port political officer, and TTSPARKS was invited to attend, along with some of the other officers on his ship. It was at this point that TTSPARKS decided to use some of his own initiative and possibly hit an intelligence home run for his new French boss, François du Bois.

Although he had never mentioned to TTSEEK or to me that he possessed a pocket-sized tape recorder (and it never occurred to us to ask about one), TTSPARKS decided to use his cassette recorder to record the political officer's remarks at the meeting. TTSPARKS knew very well that taping was absolutely forbidden at these meetings, and it was therefore very risky to attempt such a thing, but he was a cocky guy and he believed he could get away with it. And he probably would have with the proper operational guidance and the right equipment, but in this case he had neither.

His recorder was not a slick miniature that could be concealed inside of a cigarette pack; rather, it was the bulky type used to play standard music cassette tapes. It was difficult to conceal, so he just stuffed it in his jacket pocket and hoped no one would notice it. Even with all of this going against him, he might have gotten away it with it were it not for the fact that the recorder had an automatic reverse function that clacked audibly when the tape flipped to side two. And this is exactly what happened during a silent pause in the meeting.

THE INTERROGATION

When the clack-clack was heard in the room, all eyes turned toward TTSPARKS, and he was asked to identify the sound. He was arrested on the spot when he withdrew the cassette recorder from his pocket. The police then went about collecting evidence. They confiscated the cassette with the recording of the political meeting and then turned TTSPARKS's shipboard commo shack and bunk area upside down. They found the camera, several rolls of new film, and the exposed roll with the photos of the ships in the harbor. TTSPARKS was busted.

The interrogation at police headquarters lasted more than two weeks, and it was not pretty. TTSPARKS was kept in a dark, solitary cell, and the interrogation sessions were long and brutal. When his interrogators were satisfied that they had obtained all of the information TTSPARKS possessed on the subject, he was transferred to a better cell along with the general prison population and given food and permitted to sleep. He was suffering from bruises and sleep depravation and had lost several pounds, but there was no permanent physical damage. He spent the next three weeks attending reeducation seminars and security briefings in prison, and then was released and permitted to rejoin his ship when it returned to Canton.

Why was he treated so lightly? Because the police and counterintelligence officers believed his story. Why did they believe his story? Because it was credible and TTSPARKS clearly believed it. It never occurred to TTSPARKS that he was reciting a cover story during those long hours of interrogation, because TTSPARKS did not know it was a cover story. And if his interrogators strongly suspected that TTSPARKS was actually performing an intelligence-gathering mission, they clearly believed that he had been duped into it and was therefore not guilty of espionage. In the final analysis, TTSPARKS had convinced them that he was not committing espionage for a foreign country; rather, he was just an overzealous private researcher for a benign French firm with a name he couldn't pronounce—dumb perhaps, but not malicious.

THE DAMAGE ASSESSMENT

TTSPARKS phoned TTSEEK from Canton shortly after his release and relayed the story of his capture, interrogation, and subsequent release. He admitted that he gave his interrogators TTSEEK's name (an alias), the name of the company (as best he could remember it—not being a French speaker, he garbled the fictional company name), and the name François du Bois. He said he also provided physical descriptions of both TTSEEK and du Bois. Finally, he told them about the first meeting at the Seamen's Club and subsequent meetings in public places.

Thanks to the use of good clandestine tradecraft, the damage assessment showed that, aside from the phone number used by TTSPARKS to contact TTSEEK, there were no links leading back to me as the case officer or to any other assets. The operational phone number was discontinued immediately, and no safehouses, communication devices, or other special CIA equipment or personnel had been exposed. TTSEEK was instructed never to contact TTSPARKS again and, as a further precaution, all ties with TTSEEK were terminated amicably. TTSEEK was paid a healthy termination bonus and sent into happy retirement. The loss of his services as a principal agent was significant, but a serious flap had been avoided through the proper use of cover, aliases, and tradecraft.

In the end, sources and methods were protected to the extent possible despite a very serious and unfortunate security incident.

LESSONS FOR THE BUSINESS SECTOR

The protection of sources in the business arena is no different than it is in the CIA or elsewhere in the intelligence community, and it is just as important. Sun Tzu knew the importance of protecting sources 2,500 years ago. Remember, he called them the "Divine Skein," and referred to them as the treasure of a sovereign.

Let's consider again for a moment the story back in chapter 4 about the industrial espionage operation run by Volkswagen against General Motors. VW's inability to protect its source (Inaki Lopez) of information on GM's plans, designs, and programs resulted in an embarrassing and costly flap. VW got the information it was after, but its negligence in protecting Lopez led to a huge public lawsuit and finally to a settlement worth $1.1 billion.

If only the novice who directed the operation from start to finish (VW's chairman) had used some basic case officer tradecraft, he could have stolen all of those trade secrets and gotten off scot-free. Instead, he directed Lopez and his cohorts to steal boxes of documents in such a blatant fashion that the discovery of the thieves was inevitable. Furthermore, he communicated openly with his sources during the entire operation with total disregard for their security, and then compounded his agent-handling mistakes by paying the sources so lavishly that public (and police) attention was immediately focused on them. Although he followed Sun Tzu's advice by paying his sources well—"It is ten thousand times cheaper to pay the best spies lavishly, than to pay even a tiny army poorly"—he paid them openly, without any regard to their personal security.

What Lopez and his associates did was totally illegal, and they deserved to get caught and punished for their deeds. But that is not the point here. The point is that when a company engages a source of information, it should nurture and protect that source; because, like the goose that laid the golden eggs, once the source is exposed the information flow will cease.

12

CORPORATE AND FINANCIAL FRAUD

Companies can improve their financial bottom line either by making more money in the form of increased profits or by saving money by cutting costs. Losses caused by fraud and theft and the resulting litigation can come as a devastating and often unexpected blow to a company. These costs can often be avoided or at least minimized by doing some good old fashioned research before jumping into a deal with both feet. Remember the analogy of the flashlight in an unfamiliar dark room? It won't remove any of the obstacles in your way, but it will illuminate them. Do your homework before you act.

THE COST OF FRAUD

Fraud is on the rise in a variety of areas. People can acquire false identities with new names and credentials; corporations claiming to have strong track records can actually be front companies or "executive offices" without real employees; venture capitalists can pretend to be able to provide needed financing while, in reality, they are actually promoting "advance fee schemes," which only bilk companies out of large chunks of money.

Failure to conduct a thorough due diligence investigation makes it possible for unscrupulous individuals to hurt companies. Their actions, even if they are eventually caught, can leave a company in ruins.

One recent example involved a struggling telecommunications company that was approached by an investor. Since there were few strings attached to the money being offered, the company jumped at the offer of a cash infusion without bothering to check out the investor. Why bother, the company reasoned, there is nothing to lose. We can take his money at little or no risk.

However, while the investor at first offered the money with very few strings attached—one-third of the voting stock and a percentage of the return—the relationship between the company and the investor began to change rapidly. The investor became increasingly interested in the company and was given access to a significant amount of proprietary information on the running of the company, including financial records. The investor later used this information and access to transfer stock out of the name of the company president and into his own name. He then used his fraudulently acquired stock to launch a hostile takeover of the company. Once he had control of the company, he took it into bankruptcy.

After months of costly litigation, despite the evidence of fraud, the company's president was forced to settle with the thief to the tune of $3 million to get his company back.

Although the president now has regained control of his company, it cost him the $3 million he was forced to pay the investor plus an additional $3 million in legal fees. The litigation is ongoing, the bills keep mounting, and as of this writing, the company is still under Chapter 7 bankruptcy protection.

ADVANCE FEE SCHEMES

Another start-up company seeking financing met with several venture capitalists. Three of the firms were well known and well established; the fourth was a young company staffed by individuals who had worked for the more established companies but who did not yet have a track record of their own. The start-up was attracted to the young capital firm because it agreed to better terms than the established competitors and because they liked the idea of working with another young firm.

The capital firm first requested $5,000 in application fees from the start-up, explaining that it was a customary part of conducting business and that the up-front money would be "rolled in" to the amount provided to the start-up. This should have been recognized as the first warning sign that something was amiss.

The young venture capital firm continued to ask for more application fees, processing fees, and "due diligence" costs, always providing documentation from the bank or other investors indicating the deal was close to closing. The start-up also funded several European trips for the principals of the capital venture firm to visit prospective sources of funding. After the start-up paid almost $50,000 in advance fees and expenses, the venture capital firm disappeared from sight. Phones were disconnected, offices were vacated, and apartments were empty.

It later turned out that none of the individuals in the venture capital firm had any significant financing experience. They had simply fabricated their experience with the well-established firms and gambled (correctly) that no one would check. None of the money ever went toward raising capital, and all documentation concerning the search for funding was forged. The financial loss (and wasted time and energy chasing the nonexisting funding) brought the small company to its knees; the principles were forced to take second mortgages on their homes to keep the company alive.

As a general rule, whenever a potential lender asks for up-front money for any reason, you are looking at an advance fee scheme. Legitimate lenders and brokers will most certainly charge for their services, but these fees are collected when the loan is delivered—at the closing—not in advance as up-front money.

Targets for advance fee swindlers are usually individuals and companies that have had difficulty obtaining a loan through normal sources. These con artists usually offer a "guaranteed" loan, usually from a large, well-known lending institution, for a fee paid in advance. The fee is usually a percentage of the gross loan amount. The percentage usually runs around 5 percent for loans up to $1 million, with a decreasing percentage as the size of the loan goes up.

The first question to ask the loan broker is why can't you deal directly with the lending institution that supposedly will fund the loan. The answer will always be "no" for one reason or another. You may be told that the broker has a special relationship with the lender and if you try to contact them directly, it will kill the deal, or the broker will simply refuse to divulge the lender's name, citing confidentiality as the reason. The second thing to ask for is a list of other satisfied loan recipients. In this case, the swindler will either refuse to supply a list or provide you with a phony list of individuals who will vouch for him.

The bottom line is this: Any time you are asked for money up front to secure a loan and there is a degree of urgency and secrecy surrounding the transaction, you had better watch out. Once the swindler has your money, he will either disappear or keep you on the string, often asking for more and more money and giving more and more excuses why the loan is being delayed, while he bilks others like yourself.

OTHER FORMS OF COMPANY FRAUD

A couple of years ago, CTC International Group was approached by a perfume company executive who received an anonymous tip, saying one of the high-ranking officers in the company was stealing inventory and reselling it to a discount perfume outlet. We arranged for a forensic accountant to look discreetly into the possibility of theft. After several weeks of careful investigation of the company's records, a small discrepancy in an inventory list for one of the company's warehouses was noted. This led the accountant to larger inventory problems. Ultimately, the forensic accountant discovered the theft of large amounts of perfume from the warehouse by one of the vice presidents who had been hired into his position after the perfume company acquired his smaller perfume company. The company estimated the cost of the loss in the range of several million dollars.

Industrial and economic espionage, which we discussed earlier, also falls into the category of fraud.

For example, a pharmaceutical company that had spent millions of dollars and more than six years developing a drug hired a native Korean research scientist when the project was in the final stages. The scientist was U.S. educated and was considered well respected in his field. He contributed greatly to the development of the drug, but shortly before the drug was scheduled for large-scale production, South Korea announced it had developed a similar drug and would be going into production one week before the U.S. firm. The pharmaceutical company became suspicious over the Korean connection and launched its own internal investigation. The investigation revealed that the research scientist had provided all the proprietary information on the drug to the South Koreans for $75,000.

A FURTHER WORD ON FINANCIAL FRAUD

The explosive growth in the number of individuals anxious to increase their wealth by investing their extra money with high-return brokers has opened the floodgates for financial fraud. Those with knowledge of financial markets have found that it is relatively easy to set up fake investment opportunities and to recruit investors into them. They use financial lingo, invent false revenues, and create documentation "proving" their high returns. The documentation and other evidence are often so convincing that not only the inexperienced or uninformed investor is fooled, but even the savvy and knowledgeable investor can be taken. These latter individuals often become inadvertently instrumental in perpetrating the scams, because once they are brought in—often after they have conducted their own inadequate due diligence—they lend additional creditability to the swindlers perpetrating the fraud.

Despite the sophisticated methods these charlatans employ, a professional due diligence investigation almost always uncovers clues that point to fraud when it exists. At a minimum, it may show that the investment is far riskier than originally thought or portrayed. The only way to protect your investment is through professional, objective due diligence.

The huge amounts of money involved make these scams seem unreal. Some, like the well-publicized one involving Martin Frankel, receive extensive media coverage, while others remain basically secret. Many people who have been defrauded do not report their losses to authorities because they are embarrassed about being taken and believe the loss reflects badly on them. Rather than blaming the individual who set up the scam, they blame themselves for being "stupid." In fact, the scams are often so well planned and so well documented with forgeries that there is almost no way for the potential investor to verify whether the investment is real without thorough professional assistance.

In most cases, the individual behind the fraud is charming, has excellent references, is not overly pushy, and sometimes suggests the investment is exclusive. He or she may even encourage a potential investigator to do his own investigation (obviously hoping that they do not, or if they do, that the investigation will be superficial and only cover the references provided by the con man).

And if the potential investor actually does discover irregularities, the con man will happily explain them away and will be quick to suggest that they not invest if they are uncomfortable. As one individual who lost heavily stated, "He made me feel badly for doubting him. He repeatedly told me that maybe this kind of investment wasn't for me, that maybe I should look at safer, lower-return options, since I was so concerned about some of the items I had uncovered. Of course, that made me want to invest even more."

THE MARTIN FRANKEL CASE

Martin Frankel gained international attention for several reasons: the sheer amount of money he stole (initially estimated at close to $3 billion), his extravagant lifestyle, and his flight from the country, which led investigators on a merry international jet-set chase. It was good newspaper and tabloid copy.

Mr. Frankel ran a huge scam where he was supposed to invest money for several insurance companies, the Vatican, and several major insurance regulation agencies, among others. He successfully ran the scam for more than seven years by creating bogus statements to investors showing profits from the investments while he secretly moved the money offshore into his own personal accounts and to support his lavish lifestyle. Mr. Frankel did not lose the money by trading it; he never invested it in anything but his own bank accounts.

Those who invested with Mr. Frankel were stunned when they learned he had defrauded them. They universally described him as smart, charming, and funny. He was never pushy, they said, and always provided whatever documents they needed on demand.

However, as is often the case, there were clear signs (if anyone had cared to check) that Mr. Frankel was not as squeaky clean as he appeared.

As far back as 1991, he had been accused of defrauding investors and was ordered by the court to pay $975,000 in restitution. Then, in 1992, he lost his stockbroker's license and was banned from the securities industry by the SEC after investors accused him of fraud.

Mr. Frankel's most recent scam also had several red flags. The company he used was not registered or licensed, and the "corporate address" was Mr. Frankel's home. Moreover, he was spending large amounts of money on exceptionally high-priced luxury items that far exceeded his declared income. Although Mr. Frankel frequently used aliases in his new scam to obfuscate and distance himself from his previous record, there were various clues, including identical social security numbers, linking the aliases to Mr. Frankel.

One who was conned by Mr. Frankel believes he should have seen the signals that popped up during the time he was investing, but, as he put it, "Sad to say, I was blinded by greed."

STEPHEN SMITH

Stephen Smith was arrested in 1999 in Florida for running a slick "Ponzi" investment scam: While purportedly recruiting new investors for an oil well project, he was actually taking the money for himself (there was no oil well project) and using some of the money obtained from the new investors to pay dividends to earlier investors.

Mr. Smith had only been running the scam for a few months when he managed to convince several individuals in the Houston, Texas, area to invest several hundred thousand dollars in his oil well scheme. One investor noted that Mr. Smith was highly convincing and invited him to visit the wells himself. The investor did, and Mr. Smith took him on a helicopter ride of the wells and showed him immaculate records of their production and profits. The investor, who said he personally liked Mr. Smith very much after meeting him, was stunned to find out he did not own any of the wells and did not invest any money into any projects at all—oil well or otherwise. Of course, all of the records he was shown were forgeries.

Investors into Mr. Smith's recent scam also could have saved themselves a lot of money by doing some very basic research before the fact rather than waiting until after the damage had been done to check out Mr. Smith.

The after-the-fact investigation revealed that Mr. Smith had been arrested ten years earlier, in 1989, for running a similar Ponzi scheme in his native Florida. He was sentenced to fifteen years in prison after being found guilty of 19 charges of grand theft for using fraudulent financial information to obtain loans and lines of credit, 1 count of racketeering, 2 counts of organized fraud, 122 counts of the sale of unregistered securities, and 122 counts of communications fraud. In that scam, Mr. Smith defrauded approximately 700 investors out of $125 million. One of the individuals he convinced to invest in his scam was his own grandmother. He was released after serving only four years but was strictly prohibited from engaging in any financial consulting activities. Despite all of this, he couldn't resist doing it all over again, and he is now back in the slammer.

As a footnote to the story, when he was arrested in 1989, Mr. Smith had several properties in four states valued at around $1.6 million. He also had $39 million in insurance policies, seven bank accounts totaling well over $2 million, jewelry, two Mercedes automobiles, four boats, six other vehicles (including three Aston Martins), and a Rockwell International Sabreline jet plane. Additionally, he refused to cooperate with the receiver assigned to the case, despite the fact that more than $15 million from this scam was never accounted for. Although he admitted to having offshore bank accounts in

Bermuda and the Middle East, these leads were apparently never thoroughly researched, and the $15 million remains out there someplace, accessible only to Mr. Smith.

AL CUNNINGHAM

The leader of Greater Ministry International, Al Cunningham, was arrested in September 1999 for running an illegal investment Ponzi scheme and for using the money to create an armed enclave in the Caribbean. Mr. Cunningham's church offered followers a "unique opportunity" to invest in the "Caribbean market" and receive "higher than average returns."

Mr. Cunningham played up his purported religious affiliation to bring in investors. According to one person who lost several thousand dollars of his retirement money, he was hesitant to ask for references because Mr. Cunningham was "a man of the cloth." Additionally, he provided bank statements and glossy brochures to investors and frequently turned down potential investors the first time they approached him about investments. By doing this, he cleverly served to increase the desirability of his investment scheme.

According to investigators on the case, they still do not know how much money Mr. Cunningham actually stole. However, he was planning to purchase two Caribbean islands—each valued at several million dollars—and large amounts of grenade launchers, land mines, machine guns, shotguns, sniper rifles, handguns, flak vests, surveillance balloons, radar systems, and plastic explosives.

Not surprisingly, Mr. Cunningham has no legitimate religious affiliation. He made large personal purchases during the time he ran the scheme, and he has a long arrest record. This record was on file in public courthouses and was available to anyone who wanted to check. Unfortunately, no one did until it was too late for many of the investors.

OTHER CASES

Financial fraud is rampant, and the kinds of cases are only limited by the imaginations of the tricksters. Charlatans often operate internationally, to make it more difficult for U.S. authorities to catch them and to make the investment itself seem sexier.

In one recent case, an individual was coaxed into investing with an Argentinean broker who claimed to be affiliated with a well-known U.S. bank and brokerage firm. A friend of the individual had been the recipient of several years of excellent returns (a paper increase in his portfolio from an investment of $4 million to almost $13 million) from the broker, and this success spurred the new investor to jump at the opportunity.

But before giving the Argentinean broker any money, the investor decided to check him out. He visited the broker in Argentina, dined with him, visited his home and office, met his wife and kids and dog, and even met the broker's partner inside the bank where the partner claimed he worked. (Unfortunately, the bank meeting consisted of a handshake in the lobby and then off to a local restaurant for lunch. The investor never saw the banker's office, and indeed he had no affiliation whatsoever with the bank. The business card he provided was real, but it belonged to an actual bank official, not to the partner. The partner had simply adopted an alias identical to the name of a real official of the bank.)

Convinced that the operation was legitimate, the investor returned to the United States and began wiring money to the broker. Over the next two years he sent a total of $5.5 million to the broker and received statements every two weeks on the letterhead of the legitimate brokerage company and monthly bank statements on the letterhead of the legitimate bank and was in continual contact with the broker.

The broker and the investor became close friends, and the investor recommended him to a number of his friends and family, including his mother.

Two years later, when the original $5.5 million investment had purportedly reached over $11 million, the investor received an anonymous letter tipping him off that the broker was a scam artist and advising him to pull whatever money he could out of the fund immediately. The investor immediately hired an investigator, who quickly discovered that the broker and his partner had no connection to the legitimate brokerage firm or the bank, that neither were licensed to trade anything, and that all of the statements the investor had received were forgeries. The broker never invested any of the money; instead, he had stolen it all and sent it to his own offshore bank accounts. And, during the entire six years he ran the scam, his lifestyle in Buenos Aires remained low key and modest.

If he doesn't go to jail for his offenses (and he probably won't, given the cost of prosecuting crimes such as these in Argentina), the scam artist will have ample time to spend the money he has stashed away—almost $10 million from these two investors alone. And, no, none of the money was returned when the investor requested it; the only thing the investor received was three months of promises and excuses, then silence.

In yet another similar case, a Brazilian entrepreneur promised extremely high returns for a "select group of investors" on a secret project. The potential investor checked the broker's references and received enough information on the project to convince him it was a "once in a lifetime chance" and that it would succeed. Before proceeding, however, this smart investor contracted for a professional due diligence on the entrepreneur and his group. He sincerely believed the due diligence would be rote and would not show any problems (and really hoped this would be the case), but wasn't going to take any chances.

He was surprised and disappointed to learn the entrepreneur was not licensed to trade in securities, his firm was not registered, and he had previously been arrested for similar instances of investment fraud.

The list of examples is endless. It's really amazing how so many people will bicker and bargain and comparison shop for small personal items like cameras, furniture, clothing, and the like, but when it comes to spending millions of dollars on get-rich-quick investments, they can be so willing to take a tip and send their life savings to unscrupulous tricksters.

PROTECT YOURSELF FROM FRAUD

Financial fraud is definitely on the rise. For every individual who is arrested, there are many others who have never been caught or who have only recently started operating their schemes. The scams are lucrative and easier to contrive today, given the ease with which fraudulent documents can be created on a personal computer, enticing more and more criminals to enter the realm of financial fraud.

There is no way to identify a fraud from simply meeting with the principals. They are often extremely intelligent, charming, and personable. As one investor who lost several million dollars stated, "This was no used car salesman. I really liked the guy." They have the ability to manufacture extensive references and stellar credentials. Moreover, they can show reams of documentation to attest to the value of their project or strategy and will show potential investors whatever they require to convince them to invest their money in the scam.

The best way to protect yourself from fraudulent financial scams is to conduct a professional due diligence on the individuals and companies involved before sending in any money. Unless you are sure you are dealing directly with an established, reputable firm, failure to investigate up front could mean the loss of your entire investment.

REPUTATIONAL COST

In addition to the financial cost of fraud, there often is also a reputational cost to the person or company that is victimized. A damaged reputation is often at least as devastating as financial loss, and it sometimes can be more difficult to recover than mere dollars. The following are but a few examples of how reputations have been hurt by fraud.

A high-tech company hired a vice president who came highly recommended and appeared to have strong credentials. Approximately six months after he was hired, the vice president announced that he had negotiated a large sale of computer equipment to a Japanese company and an exclusive partnership arrangement with a highly reputable European company. To produce the number of items required by the Japanese, the vice president rushed production and ordered workers to skip steps, resulting in a substandard product with several built-in glitches. The Japanese returned the defective products and issued scathing statements about the company.

At the same time, the European company announced that it had no knowledge of a partnership and distanced itself from the high-tech company. Because of the poor quality of the sale to the Japanese, the company lost many of its existing contracts and had to file for bankruptcy protection. The company's reputation was further damaged by a federal investigation into stock manipulation resulting from the European partnership press announcement that had stimulated the company's stock to rise dramatically.

Although the other executives in the company were found innocent of all charges, the top three company leaders suffered so much damage to their reputations that they have not been able to find employment elsewhere in the industry or to obtain funding to start another company. Their association with shoddy workmanship and stock manipulation as a result of the vice president's actions will never be erased.

In another case, a cleaning company won the contract to clean the offices of a computer company that had several government contracts. When the computer company received a telephone call from the FBI saying someone had attempted to access a secure government site from the computer company offices, the company promised to investigate the matter. The subsequent investigation revealed that a member of the cleaning crew had "hacked" into a relatively insecure company site, which contained a list of passwords for access to government sites. The hacker then attempted to use the passwords to reach into classified sites. Although the hacker apparently never actually gained access to any classified data, and it was unclear whether he was doing it for fun—just to see if he could do it—or actually targeting classified documents, the breach of security resulted in the computer company losing its government contract and being told "off the record" that it would not be considered for any future government contracts. In the view of the U.S. government, the responsibility for maintaining proper security from its end of the operation rested squarely with the computer company.

Another example occurred when a medical company hired a new president. He claimed to have had twenty-five years of experience in the medical field and touted himself as a specialist in medical implants. After five relatively uneventful years with the company, one of the company's implants caused severe damage to a patient. The American Medical Association launched a large-scale investigation into the company and found that the president had attended only one year of medical school and had actually falsified all of his credentials and experience.

The resultant medical malpractice suits brought the company to its financial knees, but the real damage resulted from the subsequent loss of all credibility in the medical field. Even products not associated with the new president were taken off the market because of their association with the disaster.

COST OF LOST OPPORTUNITIES

Another cost that is difficult to measure is the cost of lost opportunity. For example, a U.S. utility company learned that the government of Mexico was looking for a U.S. partner. The deal seemed perfect for the U.S. utility company, but the utility had very little experience dealing with Mexico. Recognizing this weakness, the company hired a Mexican consultant whose résumé included ties to the Mexican ruling party and a high-ranking position in the state-owned utility company.

The consultant was paid a good salary and was promised a sizable bonus if the U.S. utility won the contract. After six months of intense negotiations, the Mexican government decided to partner with another U.S. company. Although disappointed at losing the contract, the U.S. utility company believed their consultant had negotiated in good faith and to the best of his ability. The company believed that the Mexican government simply made the decision to hire another company that offered them a better deal.

It was several months later that the U.S. utility company learned the Mexican government had never even considered them because Mexico had never actually received a written proposal from the U.S. utility. The company then ran a background investigation on the consultant and found that he had lied about his credentials and did not have the access he claimed to have. He was a complete charlatan.

The consultant had provided written reports and other extensive documentation that made the company believe he was actively pursuing their interests, but he was actually using the trips as paid vacations and had taken the salary without conducting any business for the utility. Despite these sizable financial costs, the chief executive of the U.S. utility believes the largest cost to the company was the lost opportunity of winning the lucrative contract with Mexico.

IDENTITY THEFT

Another growing area of fraud occurs on a more personal level. According to the Privacy Rights Clearing House, identity theft is becoming a significant problem, particularly in the United States. Identity thieves obtain personal information on unsuspecting individuals, and then—using fake drivers' licenses, credit cards, and checks—they pose as those individuals to withdraw money from their bank accounts or to purchase items on credit that they never pay for.

The individuals whose identities the criminals use are often left with ruined credit, large debts, and no way to recover their stolen money. In one recent case, two San Francisco men stole $5 million using forged documentation. Authorities arrested the men, but they have only recovered approximately $78,000. In another recent case, a convicted arsonist and murderer hid from the authorities by using the identity of the attorney who prosecuted him.

There also are numerous cases where individuals use another identity—or make up details to make themselves more interesting—which they use in relationships. For example, a woman who had been involved with a man for several years became distraught when he suddenly disappeared. She spent months trying to contact his friends and attempting to track him through his apartment and employment, with no luck.

In desperation she hired an investigator, who found out that the man had simply decided to end the relationship. He was married (and had been throughout their entire relationship) and was living only a few miles from the apartment he and the woman had used for their meetings. The apartment had been rented by the man in alias and had only been used for his extra-marital trysts.

CONCLUSION

The above stories are not aberrations. Similar incidents occur every day. The companies and individuals who fall into the swindlers' traps are usually not naïve or stupid. Most are well-seasoned, experienced businesspeople who never thought they could be fooled.

As one executive noted, his instincts had built him an empire, and he had never been wrong before; he had a perfect track record until his assistant embezzled more than $100,000 in a few months. He believes he was lucky to catch her before she did more damage. While instincts can be right 99 percent of the time, the one time they're wrong there can be disastrous consequences.

A professional due diligence investigation provides a business assessment of a company. This includes a history of the company, its operations, litigation, financial strength, reputation, profiles of key officers, and an overall assessment of the viability of the company.

A background investigation provides a similar dossier on an individual. It includes the individual's personal history, employment, civil and criminal traces, pending litigation, employment history, personal and professional reputation, financial snapshot, property, liens, judgments, bankruptcies, and assessments of character.

Be suspicious. Don't take everything at face value. And especially when there is money involved, do your homework first. Check them out.

13

EMPLOYEE VULNERABILITY

Think about it for a moment: employees are a company's only appreciable assets, yet companies often spend more time and money researching and selecting depreciable equipment than on selecting their employees. They should know that the same people they hired to support and expand growth opportunities can become potential liabilities, making them vulnerable to competitors and costly lawsuits. Enlightened employers are proactive in protecting their company by carefully selecting and managing employees. They know very well that their employees can make or break them.

One of the experts in the field of human resources is Patricia Fares of Fares & Associates, and what follows is for the most part taken directly from her advice and comments on the subject.

THE HIRING PROCESS

Ms. Fares says it all begins here, with the hiring process. Individuals with hiring authority for a company have a responsibility to hire and retain qualified, honest employees for every position, from the lowest-paid worker to the highest-level executive. Specific qualifications, including education, training, and work experience, should be determined for every position before recruitment is initiated, then job applications and résumés should be reviewed and screened to eliminate those who do not meet the minimum requirements for the job opening. Screening can also include brief telephone conversations with the applicants. This process of screening is not only cost-effective because it saves interviewing time for unqualified applicants, but it also reduces the potential legal exposure and risks related to interviewing unqualified applicants.

When the final list of basically qualified applicants is determined, interviews should be scheduled for the key individuals involved in the hiring process. All individuals conducting interviews with candidates should have a clear understanding of what constitutes legal and illegal questions that can be asked during the interview process. Many well-intentioned interviewers believe they need to know personal information about applicants in order to determine if they are the type of individual they want affiliated with their company, and this often leads to pitfalls later on.

For example, one senior executive of a large organization felt that it was important to know if an applicant was a stable, married, family person and if they attended church regularly. This executive asked all applicants these personal questions, which happens to be illegal. When one of the applicants for a key management position was interviewed by this executive and offered a job, she turned the job offer down, stating that she did not want to work for an organization that was so shortsighted in the interviewing process. She felt that ignorance of the law and insensitivity to applicants was probably representative of other executive decisions in the organization.

Much of the personal information many interviewers seek is deemed not relevant to an applicant's ability to do the job. It may also not be predictive of an applicant's work performance. Worse, these kinds of personal questions may invite lawsuits from disgruntled applicants, even when they are selected for a position in the company. Interviewers who do not have a clear understanding of the legal pitfalls of the interview process can inadvertently expose the company to discriminatory lawsuits based on questions relating to age, sex, race, religion, marital status, disability, and other areas of discrimination that are protected by law.

CHECKING REFERENCES

Ms. Fares advises that when the ideal candidate has been selected, reference checks should be conducted immediately, before any final hiring decision or job offer is made. References can offer critical work performance information that will aid in predicting the eventual success of the applicant and in identifying any potential risks or threats to other employees, customers, or vendors. Indeed, hiring laws call for a good-faith attempt to obtain work references to try to discover any potential problems for the company's other employees. Reference checks should include past employers and immediate supervisors for all of the critical positions the applicant has held during her work history.

Personal references seldom offer work performance information, so they usually add very little critical information to the reference-checking effort. Also, applicants don't usually list people as personal references who will provide any negative information on the applicant. Therefore, the employer must dig deeper to discover warts and potential problems. Full background investigations should be conducted on all key executive positions and on all employees working in sensitive areas of the company.

Ms. Fares warns that employers should also be cautious of written references provided by applicants. Letterhead from former employers is often easy to secure or copy and, consequently, work references can easily be falsified. A telephone call to the individual whose name and title appears on the written reference letter to verify the information and to ask further questions is a wise follow-up.

Approximately one-third of today's résumés and credentials have been altered or falsified. College and university degrees are often bogus, and work experience is routinely exaggerated. Verification of education is therefore very important and can be accomplished by simply calling the college or university and providing the name and social security number of the applicant. The educational institution can then verify whether a degree has been earned, and if so, the type of degree (A.A.s often become B.A.s and B.A.s often become M.A.s on résumés) and the date it was received.

Ms. Fares cited one recent case where a Fortune 500 corporation had an opening for a senior financial position in one of their division locations. The company ran ads in the local newspapers stating the major job responsibilities and experience required and noted that while a Bachelor's degree was preferred, experience would be considered in place of the degree. One of the applicants appeared ideal on the surface. He claimed to have had fifteen years of professional experience and a Master's degree from the Wharton School of Business and noted this on his application form and on his résumé. Impressed with those credentials, as well as with the candidate's technical answers during the job interview, the employer began to prepare a job offer.

During the reference check process, however, the Wharton School of Business checked its records and found that the individual had only earned a two-year Associate degree. When the applicant was confronted with the discrepancy, he stated that the degree was so old that the school records had probably not been updated. The employer admitted that this could be a possibility and asked the applicant to produce a copy of his Master's degree and a transcript record. The applicant responded by saying that his school records had been lost during a recent move and reminded the employer that a degree was not even required for the position, so it really didn't matter anyway.

Needless to say, the applicant was not hired. He had lied about his credentials. If he lied about the degree, the employer pondered, what else did he or will he lie about. It is quite simply a question of integrity.

A FINAL WORD ABOUT REFERENCE CHECKS

According to Ms. Fares, it is important that all company supervisors know that they should never provide references, verbal or written, for any current or past employee. All such requests for information on past and present employees should be referred to the Human Resources Department or other appointed individuals within the company. Only those officers who are trained in providing such references should be permitted to provide banks, lending institutions, credit card companies, schools, and potential employers with such sensitive information. Failure to do so could result in costly lawsuits. Even personnel professionals can be vulnerable and could cause problems for the company with the release of such information. Tight controls on access to this type of information is very important, and employees should be assured that their employer is in compliance.

In a recent case cited by Ms. Fares, a large high-technology company's personnel clerk received a call from an individual claiming that he was with American Express. The caller stated that one of the company's employees had applied for a larger credit line based on a recent salary increase, and that she was calling to verify the employee's current salary. The personnel clerk verified that the individual had received a raise and gave the employee's new salary and the effective date of that increase in pay. A few days later the clerk received a visit from a very angry employee. The employee informed the clerk that his wife's attorney had placed that call, and that now his wife was taking him back to court to request more alimony.

Employers should consider requiring all salary verifications be received in writing and include the requesting employee's signature of approval.

JOB OFFERS

One simple rule: Don't make promises you can't keep. Job offers, whether verbal or in writing, says Ms. Fares, should clearly state the effective date, job title, name of immediate supervisor, department, starting salary, and applicable employee benefit information. As a general rule, salary numbers should be cited for the amount the employee would receive in one paycheck, not the promise of an annualized rate. For example, if an employer pays its employees on a weekly basis and the employee is to receive $400 a week, then state that the employee's salary is $400 to be paid each week. Employers tend to make annual salary offers, which implies to some that if they are terminated after two weeks the employer still owes them another fifty weeks of pay. The offer can state that this rate, annualized, is $20,800, but it should not state that the salary offer is $20,800. This may sound overly cautious, but too many underemployed individuals can make this an issue if it is not properly written.

Employers should also beware of making any promises of advancement within the company. While it's always nice to be able to tell applicants that they have great opportunities for advancement, those conversations should be very general in nature and should not commit the company to anything.

In one case, a large manufacturing company was anxious to hire a professional they had been trying to recruit for some time. In their eagerness to get the individual to accept their offer (involving a relocation of over 2,000 miles), the manager of the department told the applicant that he would be the one to replace him as the department manager after the manager's expected promotion during the next year. The applicant accepted the position, relocated his family, and started his new job.

Over the next year, the manager came to realize that the employee was not capable of managing the department. There were also numerous complaints from other employees about the employee's unwillingness to work with the department team. So, when it came time for the manager to move up to his new position and to hire his successor, he began to look elsewhere for his replacement.

When the word of this got out, the rejected employee confronted the manager and demanded he be given the position. When he was told that he was not the right fit for the job, the employee reminded the manager that he had been promised the promotion during the hiring process. The employee demanded that he either be given the promotion or that he be laid off with one year of severance pay, continuing health benefits, and unemployment compensation benefits. He then reminded the manager that he had been induced to relocate his family with the promise of the promotion, and that he and his family had suffered in the quick relocation; his wife had left a management position, they had lost money in the sale of their home, and on and on.

The manager had given a gun to the employee and loaded it for him. Predictably, to avoid the threatened litigation, the company gave the employee everything he asked for in his settlement request. It was a very costly error.

EMPLOYMENT AGREEMENTS

Employment agreements should be considered for all sensitive and key positions in the company. The use of noncompete clauses that prohibit employees from working for or being affiliated with other competing companies for specific periods of time, in specific geographic areas, should be carefully considered. Clauses that address separation and severance payouts and continued benefit options should be carefully crafted, taking into consideration specific circumstances that might trigger any such severance benefits. Termination for cause statements, in particular, are often poorly written, according to Ms. Fares, allowing even for poor performance terminations to include liberal severance pay and ongoing, paid benefits. It is wise to consult with a qualified attorney when writing employment agreements.

NONCOMPETE AGREEMENTS

Whether included in a general employment agreement or made separately, noncompete agreements should be considered for all critical jobs, particularly software development and key positions in the high-technology industry. These agreements should restrict specific employee activities, including consorting with or becoming affiliated with a competitor, and prohibit them from unilaterally doing any sort of work for the employer's customers or competitors.

Noncompete agreements will generally have time limits of one to three years. Legal counsel should be consulted when writing employee agreements so that the company understands its ability to enforce the terms of the agreements within the current legal environment.

CONFIDENTIALITY AND NONDISCLOSURE

It is the employer's responsibility to communicate clearly to all of its employees that the protection of confidential business information is vital to the interests and the success of the company and that any violations will be pursued vigorously. Confidential information includes, but is not limited to, the following:

Financial information	Payroll information
Personnel information	Telephone information
Customer information	Alarm codes
Contract pricing	Computer security codes, source codes

Employees working with confidential information should receive regular security briefings and training to help them understand the importance of protecting confidential company information and how they should handle outside inquiries for any such information. They should be regularly reminded that any employee who discloses confidential business information will be subject to disciplinary action, including possible discharge, even if she does not directly benefit from the disclosed information. Such confidential and nondisclosure policies generally have no time limits, and employees should understand that these policies are considered perpetual.

BINDING THE COMPANY

All employees should understand that only certain of them have the authority to bind the company under any contract or to make any sort of agreements in the company's name; unless clearly authorized in writing, employees do not have the authority to bind the company through any form of verbal or written contract.

INVENTION AGREEMENTS

Invention agreements should also be considered, where appropriate. When employees work on any type of invention, including software, in the course of their employment, the rights of any inventions should be in the name of the company. Legal counsel should be consulted in the preparation of invention agreements.

POSITIVE EMPLOYEE RELATIONS

Having positive employee relations is critical for all employers. Disgruntled employees are counterproductive and can sabotage a company's work efforts.

Employee turnover is costly, regardless of labor market conditions. Studies continue to validate the direct correlation between unhappy employees, turnover, and poor management behavior.

Ms. Fares believes positive employee relations begins with the interviewing process and continues throughout employment. Clear, honest communications are key in this ongoing process. From the very beginning, the employer should communicate verbally and in writing what the employee can expect from the company and what the company expects from the employee.

Positive employee relations cannot succeed as merely a personnel slogan. It is a process of day-to-day behavior by supervisors in every function. If a company is to have committed employees, the company needs committed and sensitive leaders. Leadership is about getting people to put out their best effort consistently and helping them to grow within a motivating work environment focused on common goals and objectives.

But managing employees may also require taking disciplinary actions to resolve problem situations in the workplace in a timely and fair manner. In short, Ms. Fares urges that the fundamental principles and practices developed by a company should support positive employee relations and avoid wrongful discharge and other costly employment-related litigation.

BUSINESS ETHICS

Employers have a responsibility to maintain the highest standards of business conduct and to communicate carefully the importance of each employee's adherence to the same ethical standards while carrying out their jobs. Business ethics issues should be discussed with employees on an ongoing basis, from the time they are initially interviewed, throughout their employment, and during their exit interview. Ms. Fares believes company policies, procedures, employee handbooks, and employment agreements can be critical tools in protecting company assets and interests.

According to Ms. Fares, additional policy areas companies should consider include the following:

- **Conflicts of Interest:** Employees should be informed verbally and in writing that they have an obligation to conduct business within guidelines that prohibit actual or potential conflicts of interest. An actual or potential conflict of interest occurs when an employee is in a position to influence a decision that may result in a personal gain for that employee or for a relative as a result of the company's business dealings.

Employees should also be told that no presumption of impropriety is created by the mere existence of a relationship with outside firms. However, if an employee has any influence on transactions involving purchases, contracts, or leases, it is imperative that he or she disclose to the appropriate executive of the company as soon as possible the existence of any actual or potential conflict of interest so that safeguards can be established to protect all parties. Personal gain may result not only in cases where an employee or an employee's relative has a significant ownership in a firm with which the company does business, but also when that person receives a kickback, bribe, substantial gift, or special consideration as a result of any transaction or business dealings involving the company. It is critical that employees also understand that the materials, products, designs, plans, ideas, computer source codes, financial information, customer lists, pricing policies, and other data of the company are the property of the company and should never be given to an outside firm or individual except through normal channels and with appropriate authorization.

- **Conduct and Work Rules:** To ensure orderly operations and provide the best possible work environment, employees should be expected to follow rules of conduct that will protect the interests and safety of all employees, customers, and vendors. Employees should be expected to observe reasonable standards of job performance and good conduct, including attendance, work performance, courtesy, and adherence to safety and other workplace policies. When performance or conduct does not meet standards, the company should first endeavor to provide the employee with a reasonable opportunity to correct the problem. If this doesn't work, progressive disciplinary policies and procedures should be considered.

SEXUAL HARASSMENT

Some years ago a couple of female CIA reports officers had a sign taped to the door of their office. It read in large block letters: "SEXUAL HARASSMENT WILL NOT BE TOLERATED." And in smaller letters at the bottom of the sign it read: "but it will be graded."

That was the prevailing attitude back then. It was a fun subject to be joked about. Not so today. Sexual harassment in the workplace has existed since time immemorial, but today employers are forced to deal with the problem under penalty of law. It has been mandated as part of the Title VII Civil Rights Act that every person has the legal right to work in an environment free from harassment on the basis of sex.

While sexual harassment receives most of the media attention, harassment based on race, color, religion, national origin, age, disability, and other areas protected by law also constitutes unlawful harassment in the workplace. Harassment in the workplace affects everyone at all levels and in all types of jobs. It affects productivity, produces emotional stress, and causes morale problems, turnover, and, often, legal expenses.

Employers must take steps to eliminate all forms of harassment in the workplace to protect their company. Clear policies and procedures must be written and distributed to all employees. Ms. Fares advises that employees should also attend training workshops to ensure that they understand the policies, procedures, employer's expectations, and consequences of noncompliance.

All complaints of harassment should be promptly and thoroughly investigated by a trained professional. Remedial action must be taken swiftly, and retaliation against any employee filing a good-faith claim must not be permitted under any circumstances.

Creating an environment free from any kind of harassment is a responsibility that is shared by the employer and the employees.

EMPLOYMENT TERMINATION

Exit interviews should be scheduled for all departing employees, regardless of why they are terminating the employment relationship. The exit interview can afford an opportunity to discuss employee benefits, conversion privileges, return of employer-owned property, and many other subjects, including the performance of coworkers and supervisors.

Suggestions, complaints, and questions should be discussed, as well as the critical confidential and disclosure policies and the employment agreement and noncompete clause that the employee may have signed when first employed.

RETURN OF PROPERTY

Employees should understand that they are responsible for all property, including any computer, alarm, and telephone codes, identification cards, charge cards, tools, uniforms, keys, beepers, cell phones, computers, materials, work orders, handbooks, and other written information issued to them or in their possession or control. Employees must return all property of the employer that is in their possession or control in the event of termination of employment or immediately upon request for any reason whatsoever.

POLICIES AND PROCEDURES

In summary, Ms. Fares recommends that all of the policies and procedures listed below be considered for use when dealing with any employee:

- Employee handbook
- Operating policies and procedures
- Reference checks
- Background investigations
- Employment agreements
- Noncompete agreements
- Invention agreements
- Conflict of interest policy
- Confidential and nondisclosure information
- Conduct and work rules
- Antiharassment, sexual harassment policy
- Employment termination policy
- Property assignments
- Job offers

Employees should be as aware of the rules and regulations governing their personal conduct in the workplace as they are about what is expected of them in performance-related activities. Disgruntled or unhappy employees can cause companies irreparable harm when the "revenge" motive moves them to act against a company. In the next chapter we will examine how negative forces at work within the CIA almost brought that proud organization to its knees a few years ago.

14

CIA DEFECTORS: HOW COULD THEY DO IT?

When the news broke of yet another former colleague's arrest on charges of spying, I got a sinking feeling in the pit of my stomach. When will it all end? Like a boxer long past his prime, the CIA was reeling from the continuous barrage of jabs from the press, Congress, and elsewhere over alleged drug dealing, misdeeds in Central America, and other spurious attacks. Powerful hooks and uppercuts had been delivered by the betrayals of the likes of Aldrich Ames and, more recently, by another case officer named Harold J. Nicholson. How could this happen? How could a trusted officer of the CIA betray his country, his colleagues, and this once-proud Agency? A review of the years since the birth of the CIA offers clues to the answer, and an analysis of what happened offers some very important lessons to be learned for the business sector.

THE WAY IT USED TO BE

When I was recruited off of my college campus into the CIA in the mid-1960s, the Agency was a growth business. The Vietnam conflict was in full swing and the Agency's leadership consisted of seasoned veterans of the Office of Strategic Services (OSS) and World War II. These men and women, then in their fifties, held virtually every senior CIA post in the field and at Head-quarters, and had played musical chairs with those top positions since the Agency's establishment in 1947. They were a proud, aloof group of colorful heroes who instilled their values of "honor, duty, country" in those junior officers who followed them. The CIA was a closed, secretive society, well insulated and protected from outside attacks. "No comment" was the most that ever escaped the Agency's lips when questioned by the press. Oh yes, and the much-maligned "old-boy" network was in full force. These legendary leaders protected each other and their protégés, and the loyalty they displayed downward was rewarded by devotion, trust, and similar loyalty upward. The mere thought that a member of such a select fraternity would betray its code of conduct was unheard of: it simply couldn't happen here; not in this environment, not with this leadership.

THE FIRST BLOW

But as the CIA aged, things inevitably began to change. The first serious blow to the organization occurred in 1973, when James Schlesinger, an outsider, was brought in to take over the reigns of the proud CIA family. He was ambitious, unschooled in the arcane business of intelligence, and really only accepted the job as a stepping-stone to the position of secretary of defense anyway. In the short year of his tenure as DCI (Director of Central Intelligence), he decimated the ranks of senior management (the "old boys") through a contentious reduction in force exercise and threw open the Agency's doors to censure from the outside. With the veil of secrecy lifted, the Agency suddenly became vulnerable to outside criticism. For the first time, it was on the defensive, and Schlesinger's successor, Bill Colby, was left to deal with the mess he had inherited. And then Colby just made things worse with his misguided policy of openness to the press. The standard, "No comment" became, "Come look at us. We're an open book."

Soon Congress was investigating every alleged mistake and misdeed the Agency had ever been accused of in its entire thirty-year history. The CIA withdrew to lick its wounds, while employee initiative and morale plummeted. Case officers, station chiefs, and managers back at CIA headquarters in Langley were afraid to take even the slightest operational risks for fear something would go wrong; that a "flap" would occur. The punishment for failure was far worse than the reward for achievement, and the result was that the quality of human intelligence produced by the Agency plummeted and new operations were routinely declared too risky to undertake. One colorful senior station chief described it as "masturbation without ejaculation." Case officers were permitted to spot, assess, and develop new agent talent, but if there was the slightest risk that the target might refuse the recruitment pitch and would report it, permission to proceed with the operation would be withheld. Bugging operations were permitted to run through the casing and planning stages, but once it came time to plant the bug, the risk of detection was usually declared to be too great and the operation was canceled at the last minute. This was the beginning of the decline.

THE WORST WAS YET TO COME

The next disaster occurred a few years later, in 1977, when President Jimmy Carter appointed his Naval Academy buddy, Admiral Stansfield Turner, to the post of DCI. Turner came to the Agency with the belief that the CIA's emphasis on human collection activities was an obsolete concept and that technical collection methods were the only way to go in the future. He also believed that what CIA operations officers were doing was immoral (recruiting and handling unsavory spies) and that they must therefore be personally immoral as well. So, as a prelude to another massive purge of the CIA's ranks, he launched an absurd and insulting witch-hunt to investigate the moral behavior of its case officers. He sent his close friend, Rusty Williams, another Naval Academy buddy, to CIA stations around the globe with orders to delve deeply into the personal and professional lives of the case officers. One of the things he found was a particularly high divorce rate among CIA case officers and, predictably, he attributed this more to loose morals rather than the stress, long hours, and dangerous nature of their work. The purges began in force when Rusty Williams returned to Washington, and Turner announced that henceforth only "patriots" would be recruited; case officers should no longer recruit venal turncoats who were motivated solely by revenge and money.

It took about a year for Turner to realize just how wrong he was, and to his credit, he did try to rectify his mistakes and rebuild the decimated operations directorate, but too many babies had already been thrown out with the bathwater. The damage to the Agency's morale and public image had been done, and the stage was set for the first known foreign penetration of the CIA: In 1980 a case officer named David Barnett pleaded guilty to spying for the Soviet Union while serving in Indonesia. The unthinkable had happened. The CIA's inner sanctum had been penetrated for the first time, and morale within the Agency plummeted even further.

Things improved for a short time in the early 1980s under President Ronald Reagan's new DCI, Bill Casey. But new scandals related to events like Iran-Contra started things spiraling downward once again from the mid-1980s on, and other employee defections followed as attacks mounted.

The year 1985 was particularly bad for the Agency: Former journeyman case officer Edward Lee Howard fled the country as he was about to be arrested by the FBI for passing secrets to the KGB, and Sharon Scranage, a CIA operational support assistant assigned to Accra, Ghana, was convicted of passing classified information to the Ghanaian Intelligence Service. This also was the year that Aldrich Ames began his traitorous association with the Soviet Union, and the year before CIA translator Larry Wu-Tai Chin was convicted of passing secrets to the Chinese Intelligence Service. Chin suffocated himself in his cell rather than face a long prison sentence.

HITTING ROCK BOTTOM

By the early 1990s, the Agency had sunk to an all-time low in terms of morale, mission, and leadership. Talented officers at the upper- and middle-management ranks began bailing out in unprecedented numbers, as a succession of mediocre, unschooled DCIs came and went. The trend continued well into the mid-1990s, and the prevailing negative atmosphere contributed to yet another major defection. It wasn't a great surprise when, no sooner than the dust had settled from the devastating Ames case, another one popped up: Harold Nicholson, a bright, middle-level case officer who was being groomed for senior management positions in the Agency, was arrested and charged with betraying his country to Russia for a paltry $180,000.

MOTIVATING FACTORS

With all of this said, only part of the blame for these CIA defections can be attributed to the erosion of loyalty among its officers and the loss of public trust and confidence in the organization. Convincing a member of one intelligence service to spy for another is the ultimate in salesmanship, and it is a highly personal process. It involves an in-depth assessment of the potential recruit's vulnerabilities and motivations, leading to the offer of rewards based on that assessment. While Nicholson, Ames, and the rest all received monetary compensation for their cooperation, money alone is almost never the sole motivation for treason. Sure, a spy will almost always accept money in return for providing state secrets, and this is good for building control into the operation, but there is always a stronger, deeper, more personal motivation that leads them over the edge to commit treason.

Revenge is the prime motivator, and there are others as well. The desire for recognition not provided by the Agency, wanting to "stick it" to the organization and/or specific supervisors who had wronged the officer or didn't promote him fast enough, the officer wanting to show that he can get away with it—that he is smarter than "they" are, or just the thrill of seeing if he can get away with it—for the adrenaline rush.

One thing is certain: none of these people thought they would get caught. But they did, and at least in the cases of Ames and Nicholson, they got caught because they were incredibly stupid. They forgot the first lesson of Clandestine Tradecraft 101: they lived beyond their means; they spent the ill-gotten rewards of their betrayals.

LESSONS FOR THE BUSINESS SECTOR

No company can avoid defections. No matter how many benefits are offered, and how much money is paid out in salaries and bonuses (witness the GM to VW defections we discussed earlier), there will still be those who can be persuaded that the grass is greener elsewhere. Loyalty is not something that can be bought solely with material incentives. When an employee leaves one company for another, as most will inevitably do, they will take with them all of the knowledge and experience they gained in the previous company. This too cannot be avoided. But there are some basic things that can be done to limit the losses to a company through theft—both information theft and material theft—and lawsuits. Most of them are common sense and have been discussed in previous chapters, but it is worthwhile to quickly review them here.

SELECT EMPLOYEES CAREFULLY

The first thing is to try to weed out the bad apples at the front end, before they are hired. Background investigations should be run on every new employee before they are hired. While background checks on lower-paid workers can, for the most part, be limited to simple, inexpensive criminal checks (people who have stolen before are more likely than others to steal again), candidates for middle- and upper-management positions deserve closer scrutiny. Here it is important to look at the whole package. Integrity issues such as honesty and trustworthiness should be examined closely. After all, these are the managers who are the face of the company; these are the people who deal with suppliers and clients; these are the individuals who are given the responsibility to handle the company's purse strings; these are the ones who will make or break a company.

The ability to work with others is crucial for most positions. As with the CIA example, when morale is high, loyalty tends to be high and production follows. When it falls, disgruntled employees are more likely to take revenge on a company, and the results can be very costly.

An examination of a prospective employee's financial history can provide clues to how they will handle the affairs of the company; people who can't handle their own personal affairs can rarely handle a company's. Also, people with money problems are more likely to cheat than others.

Previous work performance and personality traits that may affect performance must be given special attention. And this information may be very hard to come by through normal interviews with former employers that are listed on an applicant's résumé. Most companies are extremely reluctant to make any negative comments about a previous employee for fear of being sued. Indeed, many employees who have been fired for cause insist on having statements written into their termination agreements that preclude the company from stating the reasons for termination.

TERMINATION CLAUSES

In a recent case, a high-tech company in Silicon Valley hired a new chief financial officer (CFO) whose résumé indicated he was highly qualified for the position. When, after only a few short months on the job, the CFO's performance and negative attitude became untenable, the company contracted for a belated background investigation.

The investigation showed that the CFO had actually been fired from three previous companies listed on his résumé as well as from a fourth company he neglected to list on his résumé (omissions of this sort are as important as embellishments). And all of the firings were for exactly the same problems that the CFO exhibited with the Silicon Valley company.

The CFO had agreements not to disclose the reasons for his termination with each of the three companies he had included on his résumé. (This was why the routine reference checks didn't reveal the problems.) But, predictably, he did not have this kind of agreement with the company he had left off his résumé.

Needless to say, if the company had had this information before the CFO was hired, the hiring would never have taken place. Instead, the company was forced to honor its contract and provide the CFO with a year's salary and a sizable termination bonus to get rid of him. And, yes, you guessed it, the termination agreement forbids the company to mention the reasons for the firing.

The conclusion for the business sector is clear: the only way to avoid defections, lawsuits, lowered productivity, revenge resulting in the theft of trade secrets, and a myriad of other possible business-wrecking actions is to select your employees carefully at the outset and then to provide them with a work environment that is both rewarding and challenging. Stir in a management style that encourages loyalty from the top down and the company will be in harmony. Once the employees see that management is prepared to stand behind them, their loyalty toward management will be inspired and mutual trust will be assured.

Part 4

TERRORISM AND OTHER
DANGERS ABROAD

15

INTERNATIONAL TERRORISM: GOING FROM BAD TO WORSE

The cold war is over. The Soviet Union has collapsed from within. The Russian bear has been slain and skinned and the specter of nuclear annihilation and mutually assured destruction (MAD) has passed.

But it's still a very rough neighborhood out there, particularly for large U.S. and Western corporations.

In fact, it is probably worse now than ever before in recent history. The conventional forces of our erstwhile enemies may no longer be a threat, but new Iraqi antagonists, whose own relatively meager conventional capabilities were mutilated during Desert Storm and Desert Fox, are busy sharpening their weapons of terrorism—their only remaining viable means of counterattack against the U.S. and Western governments and economies. And Iraq is not the only Islamic antagonist wanting to stick a spear into the "Great Satan," as witnessed by the 11 September 2001 kamikaze attacks on the World Trade Center and Pentagon. Others have both the desire and capabilities, and they would be happy to join in and implement their own successful terrorist attacks against the United States and its allies.

The combination of the Soviet collapse and rise of Islamic militarism in the Middle East is creating a harrowing scenario of a long-term global terrorist war directed against the Western nations.

TERRORISM IS ALL THAT REMAINS

First, a strong, united Soviet Union has been replaced by anarchy in Eastern Europe. The glue that held these disparate nations together has dried and cracked and the union has crumbled. Nationalistic former allies are bickering, their economies are in shambles, people are frustrated, military forces are in disarray. Antidemocracy sentiment and jealousy directed toward the West are reemerging. And the bankrupt former Red Army is selling its bullets and its guns and its explosives and its missiles and its plutonium. The United States has identified more than fifty nation-states that are of concern as suppliers, conduits, or potential proliferators of nuclear materials and armaments that can be brought to bear against the United States in one form or another.

Second, Islamic fundamentalism, with an increasingly hostile Iraq in the vanguard, is fueling anti-Americanism in the Middle East. The supporters of terrorism (Syria, Iran, Iraq, Libya, Sudan, Afghanistan and its guest Osama bin Laden, and others) now have a bazaar full of cheap weapons and munitions from which to select. And if they don't already know how, information on how to build a nuclear bomb, or to cook up a batch of sarin gas, or to turn farmyard cow chips into anthrax is readily available in public libraries and on the Internet.

The CIA has stated that a number of supranational terrorist organizations are actively seeking to procure or develop chemical and biological weapons, and about a dozen states hostile to the Western democracies, including Iran, Iraq, Libya, North Korea, and Syria, now either possess or are actively pursuing offensive biological and chemical capabilities. For example, the terrorist Osama bin Laden has shown a strong interest in chemical weapons and has trained his operatives on how to conduct attacks with toxic chemicals or biological toxins.

THE TERRORIST HAS THE ADVANTAGE

To make matters worse, the terrorist has all the advantages. He is free to choose the weapons, to choose the battlefields, to choose the time of attack, and to select attackers from an ever-growing pool of United States–hating fanatics. The terrorist is the aggressor; we are on the defense. The threat of nuclear, biological, and chemical terrorism is the greatest challenge facing Western intelligence communities today. And it only takes one shadowy martyr to inflict terrible damage; not an army. It is indeed a rough neighborhood out there, and things are going to get rougher before they get better.

The main line of defense for the United States against international terrorism is the CIA. The Agency places counterterrorism at the top of its priority requirements and, in fact, has had greater success in the area than any other intelligence organization. Unfortunately, that success has not been consistent or widespread enough to provide adequate early warning of impending terrorist attacks. Why? Because the best information on terrorist plans and intentions must come from human source (that is, real people, real spies) information, and those sources come from within such a closed group that they are not easily accessible or penetrable. Terrorist organizations are the single hardest intelligence target to penetrate with human sources. Advances in technical collection methods (SIGINT, ELINT, imagery) have not compensated for the lack of HUMINT in this area.

RECRUITING TERRORISTS

The recruitment of new agent sources is the main task of the CIA case officer, and one of the most important courses taught to new operations officers at the Farm is "The Recruitment Cycle." (We discussed this at length in the chapter on recruitment.) This is a basic "how-to" course describing the steps and techniques required to induce the in-place defection of new sources of intelligence.

Recall that the recruitment cycle involves four distinct phases: spotting, assessing, developing, and delivering the final recruitment pitch. In short, the course teaches the new officers how to *spot* new agent talent (that is, find people with access to the information desired); how to *assess* their susceptibility to recruitment; how to use their perceived susceptibilities, vulnerabilities, and desires to massage and *develop* them to the point of recruitment; and then how to design and *deliver* a recruitment pitch based on the personal information obtained. Inducements of money, recognition, and revenge are examples of major motivators; most spies accept recruitment to gain one or more of these things.

But the terrorist target is different.

A few years ago, as a CIA operations officer tasked with recruiting penetrations of terrorist organizations abroad, I often longed for the days when my recruitment targets could be approached and developed in civilized settings like embassy cocktail parties, diplomatic picnics, tennis tournaments, and the like. While these venues are appropriate for spotting most foreign intelligence targets, not so with the terrorist.

When a CIA case officer targets an international terrorist organization for penetration, the first step is to examine its membership. Up until the 11 September attacks, the profile of an international bomb-planting terrorist was an Arab male between the ages of seventeen and twenty-four, raised in the strict Muslim faith in a small rural Middle Eastern town (somewhere like the remote Bekáa Valley of Lebanon); harboring a deep hatred of the West, and the United States in particular; and possessing a fanatical willingness to martyr himself in the name of Allah. He was highly suspicious of all foreigners, had few if any foreign-language skills, and shunned anyone who was not of his Muslim faith, clan, and heritage. The 11 September kamikaze bombers generally met this profile, with the exception of the education and language skills. These terrorists were living in our midst in the United States and spoke English.

Furthermore, the terrorist usually doesn't frequent any of the traditional agent-spotting arenas for the CIA and other intelligence agencies: he doesn't usually hang out in bars or frequent upscale restaurants, is not to be found on the diplomatic circuit, nor on tennis courts or golf links, or at cultural events, or at any of the other usual spots where case officers would normally troll for prospective agents. The suspicious, shadowy terrorist and the urbane case officer simply do not move in the same circles.

ALTERNATIVE METHODS

You see the problem. The CIA's recruitment doctrine is not entirely germane when dealing with the terrorist target. The terrorist can't be recruited if the CIA case officer is not in a position to spot, assess, and develop him first. So the CIA case officer must step back and work through intermediaries, or *access agents,* as they are called in the trade. Remember that an access agent is one who bridges the gap between the target and the case officer. He is directed by the case officer to spot, assess, and develop potential recruits in the terrorist milieu. But finding such an intermediary is a momentous task in and of itself. The gap between the urbane American case officer and the Arab militant is still too great to bridge in one step. So additional links in the chain, additional access agents, must be added, further distancing the CIA case officer from his target, and exponentially compounding the difficulty of the operation.

Sometimes there are several links in the chain from the case officer to the actual terrorist operative. The chain might look something like this: case officer to wealthy Arab businessman, to small Arab shopkeeper in Lebanon, to the shopkeeper's relative in the Bekáa Valley, to the relative's friend on the fringes of the terrorist organization, to the terrorist himself.

Then, assuming the CIA case officer is able to orchestrate such a daisy chain, there are the problems of getting accurate and timely information up the chain to the case officer, and requirements down to the terrorist recruit.

THE ETHICAL ENIGMA

But that's not all. Let's assume for a moment that the case officer is successful in recruiting and running a penetration of a terrorist organization. He or she must now struggle with the problem of handling such an unsavory character; a person who is prepared to kill innocent civilians and who may have killed before. The legal and ethical questions that arise from this are mind-boggling. And to take this even one step further, what if the operation produces intelligence that warns us of an impending act of terrorism? Clearly we could not permit the act to take place, so the authorities would have to be called in to thwart the act and to arrest the perpetrators. That would blow the entire operation, including our penetration, and we would be left back at ground zero, having to spot, assess, develop, and recruit another source who would, in turn, last only as long as the first bit of critical intelligence he provides.

All this is not to say that the CIA should give up trying to penetrate terrorist organizations, or that it has not had some (mostly unheralded) successes in the past against the terrorist target. It is only to say that the task is indeed a gigantic one, and the CIA will require new thinking and some unique approaches to be successful. In the meantime, U.S. and Western interests, both at home and abroad, will remain increasingly vulnerable to terrorist attack.

A PRIME EXAMPLE

The ongoing debate between intelligence producers and intelligence customers, particularly between the CIA and the State Department, concerning the use of sensitive intelligence to advance political goals, reached contentious new heights a little over ten years ago. The following story is illustrative of how the pressures to act on intelligence can result in the deaths of the very agents who produce it, particularly when dealing with the elusive terrorist target.

According to an explosive article written by Michael Wines that appeared in the *New York Times* on 7 February 1991, two or three intelligence agents—native Palestinians who had penetrated a major terrorist group in Lebanon—were uncovered and executed in the fall of 1990 following a rare diplomatic démarche made to President Hafez Assad of Syria by then secretary of state James Baker and several other State Department officials. Syria's foreign minister, Farouk al-Sharaa, and several lower-ranking Syrian officials also attended the meeting.

The démarche, delivered on 14 September 1990, concerned Syria's support of Palestinian terrorists located in Lebanon, most likely in the Bekáa Valley, where several terrorist organizations had their training camps, and in Beirut, where it was thought American hostages who had been kidnapped there (Associated Press journalist Terry Anderson, the Reverend Benjamin Weir, the CIA's Beirut station chief William Buckley, and others) were being held by the terrorist group Hezbollah. It reportedly included unusually detailed information about U.S. knowledge of terrorist activities in the region, including evidence of Syria's direct involvement in supporting terrorist groups.

According to the article, the United States first learned about the agents' deaths in November or December 1990 but went to great lengths to keep the news secret because it raised the question of whether Syria deliberately misused the privileged information to assist a terrorist group it was supporting. The article quoted several U.S. officials as saying they strongly suspected a direct link between the Assad briefing and the deaths of the agents.

The officials said that the actual meeting was preceded by a sharp debate between intelligence experts and State Department officials over how strongly the United States should confront Assad with its evidence of Syrian involvement in terrorism. The State Department argued that Assad should be given an unusually detailed briefing about the actions of Syrian-supported terrorists to impress upon him the weight of the evidence against his government. Conversely, the intelligence officials argued that such a briefing would put undercover agents and methods of collecting information at risk.

One official was quoted as saying: "It was quite an argument. The intelligence guys finally told them, 'Okay, but the blood will be on your hands if something happens.'"

In the end, the State Department won. And apparently it threw caution to the wind and went too far in its briefings of Assad; it just couldn't help showing Assad just how well informed it was concerning the terrorists' intentions and capabilities, despite the risk it posed to the agents involved—the sources of the information.

Predictably, the State Department has remained defensive on the subject. When pressed for an answer to the "coincidence" of the executions following so closely on the heels of the Assad briefing, one State Department spokeswoman refused to confirm that any deaths had even taken place. However, when pressed for an alternate explanation for what happened, she said that the United States had received a "credible and serious threat against an American ambassador in the region last year, and had acted on it." She added: "Any démarche that may have been passed on such a subject would have been done solely to protect the life of an American ambassador and would be fully coordinated within this Government, including our intelligence community." She refused to admit even the possibility that the Assad/Baker démarche had anything at all to do with the deaths of the agents.

So, when is it permissible to give up a source in order to act on an intelligence report? The State Department's spokeswoman suggests that if the intelligence information concerns something as serious as a possible attack on a U.S. ambassador, then a démarche to the government detailing the intelligence reporting (and thereby risking the lives of the sources) is okay, but if it concerns a more general form of terrorism, as in the Assad/Baker case, the démarche would be far less detailed in an effort to protect the sources involved. The spokeswoman said: "Any suggestion that Secretary Baker handed over a démarche that led to the death of any individual is categorically untrue." The implication then is that the Baker démarche was therefore a bland one, and that no sensitive sources or methods were revealed.

In those days, the pressure on the intelligence community (particularly the CIA) from the White House and the State Department to obtain information on the welfare and whereabouts of the notorious hostages being held in Beirut was intense. There was no higher intelligence priority than this. Unfortunately, those terrorists holding the hostages knew very well that the U.S. government was using every means at its disposal to obtain this information, so they were very careful to keep it from us. The hostages were moved from place to place regularly under cover of darkness, their guards were carefully screened and only the most trusted people were used for this purpose, the need-to-know principle was exercised religiously so that most people living in the buildings where the hostages were kept did not know they were there, and all of those involved in the handling of the hostages knew that swift death would come to anyone who divulged any information concerning them.

Since it was well known that Syria was the major supporter of Hezbollah (the Party of God), the group that was holding the hostages, it is likely that this was precisely the kind of information that was discussed during the meetings with Assad.

The strange request to brief the leader of a country known to support terrorism had sprung from a desire by the State Department to confront Assad with evidence that terrorist acts were being planned and executed from territory controlled by Syria and by a group receiving aid and assistance from Syria.

TARGET SELECTION

Now add this to the equation: In addition to the terrorists' many advantages already mentioned, they have an endless supply of potential targets, ranging from the most difficult to the easiest, to choose from. The reason Osama bin Laden chose to attack the U.S. embassies in Nairobi and Dar Es Salaam over other more lucrative embassies was their relative vulnerability. While official U.S. installations abroad (embassies, consulates, military bases, and so forth) top the list of terrorist targets, some are virtual fortresses while others have very little security. However, regardless of their security level, all are symbolic of the United States and fly the Stars and Stripes above their installation.

In a perverse way, the very efforts of the U.S. State Department to beef up the security of U.S. embassies and other official installations abroad make the facilities of IBM, American Airlines, EXXON, Coca-Cola, American Express, even McDonalds, more attractive to the terrorist. You see, when terrorists find security too tight on their preferred targets, they simply move down the priority list to "softer" targets. If they have to move from an official target to a nonofficial target, so be it; as long as an installation has a symbolic American flag flying over it, it is a target. This is why PanAm 103 was selected as a target and blown out of the air by Libyan terrorists.

WHAT THE FUTURE HOLDS

Thus, when the relative impotence of our intelligence and law enforcement agencies is weighed against the seeming omnipotence of terrorist organizations, we have to wonder what the future holds for the United States and its allies—in both official and nonofficial capacities. If we didn't believe it before the 11 September terrorist attacks on the World Trade Center and the Pentagon, it has now become abundantly clear that we are no longer safe from terrorism, at home or abroad. U.S. and Western companies, particularly the airlines, are forced to deal with the problem of international terrorism as a part of the risk in doing business anywhere.

LESSONS FOR THE BUSINESSMAN

Terrorism has become a fact of life, particularly for those companies and businesspeople who operate in the international arena. The problem must be dealt with reasonably and effectively by everyone who boards an aircraft or walks the streets of Moscow, Algiers, Paris, or even New York. Security can be expensive and intrusive. But the answer is not to stick our heads in the sand and pretend there is no problem. Our governments can't offer much more assistance than providing us with routine travel advisories and security briefings and the like. Also, as noted above, the mere fact that official government installations abroad are beefing up their security has a perverse affect on private representative installations overseas. In the next chapter we will examine some commonsense things travelers can do to avoid becoming a terrorist target in the international environment.

16

DOING BUSINESS ABROAD

A few simple precautions will decrease your chances of being the victim of a terrorist or criminal attack while traveling abroad. While the tourist can pick and choose the countries and locations within the countries to visit, this is not the case with the business traveler. The businessman must go where the business is. The best advice I can give is to do your homework on the place you intend to visit before you embark on a trip, and then to remain alert and use good common sense once you get there.

THE BACKGROUND SITUATION REPORT

Let's say your business brings you to Bogota, Colombia, and you have never visited the country before. The first step would be to learn a bit about the country and the specific risks travelers face when they visit. The best place to start is the State Department's website (http://www.state.gov). There you can click on the country you are planning to visit and learn everything from basic background demographic information, climate, cultural peculiarities, visa requirements, and shots required down to a list of security incidents that have occurred in the country during the past several years. More detailed and fulsome reports, similar to the one in which the following information on Colombia has been extracted, can be obtained from a number of security firms specializing in providing this sort of information.

Some general helpful hints will be listed in the reports. For example, because of the very high crime rate in Colombia, travelers would be advised not to carry unneeded cash or travelers checks or credit cards outside of the hotel. Other suggestions would include carrying a photocopy of your passport's first three pages instead of carrying the passport itself, not to display expensive watches or jewelry, and to select taxis carefully and never to enter one with more than the driver inside. Never accept candy, cigarettes, or beverages of any kind from a stranger, because they may contain knockout drugs. Get through airport formalities quickly on departure and move briskly to the departure lounge rather than amble through the airport. In other words, trust your instincts and remain alert.

Because of the threat of kidnappings, muggings, and other criminal activities in Bogota, you would be advised to alter your daily pattern as much as possible while traveling around the city. Strangers, or others without a need to know, should not have access to your travel plans during your stay. The reports would suggest that you travel in-country only during daylight hours, and that you stay on the main highways. Traveling by train or public bus would be discouraged, as well as traveling alone. You would be advised that lodgings should be selected carefully and reservations double-checked. The reports might also go so far as to suggest using a travel alarm door lock on hotel room doors and to select rooms above the third floor whenever possible. You might be advised to check the locks on windows and balcony doors as well. The reports also may suggest that you be careful of what you eat and drink. In addition to the Mickey Finn threat, cholera cases are increasing in Colombia, and the two national mineral water companies have been found to have contaminated plants.

You would be advised to consider all cities in Colombia as dangerous, with Bogota, Cali, and Medellin being especially bad. Travel to the border regions would be discouraged, and the traveler would be advised to be aware that vast areas of the country are void of any police or military presence. Armed escorts would be advised if you were forced to travel to the remote regions.

If you intended to reside in Bogota, you would be advised that it would be prudent to live in an apartment, as opposed to a house or villa, because they are much easier to make secure than detached dwellings. The U.S. embassy recommends selecting an apartment above the third floor and suggests avoiding penthouses, because intruders can more easily gain access from adjoining or nearby rooftops. You would be told that all glass should be treated with Mylar to reduce shattering in the event of a bomb blast, and that the apartment should have armed guards as well as a reliable video and alarm system. Additional precautions might suggest that entry doors should be dead-bolted and reinforced with steel, and that steel grills should be installed on windows and glass doors. The U.S. embassy goes so far as to suggest that dwellings in Bogota include a well-stocked safe-haven area with the following accessories: battery-operated radio and telephone, water, food, fire extinguisher, first aid kit, alarm system, grilles, and rape gate (a steel gate covering the door). If you are qualified to handle one, a weapon, preferably a shotgun with extra ammunition, would also be handy.

Burglaries and armed intrusions can be minimized in all areas of the world by practicing good defensive measures faithfully. The first precaution is to investigate carefully your personal servants and to have the doormen and other employees with access to the building checked out. Virtually all burglaries and intrusions reported by the foreign business and diplomatic communities over the past few years have been "inside" jobs, that is, collusion between the robbers and the maid or doorman, or both. At times, even the security guards have been found to be in cahoots with the burglars. Your residence should never be left unattended—ever. Someone—gate guard, maid—should always be on the premises. And family and servants should be taught how to handle conversations with strangers, especially so-called wrong number calls.

Multinational corporations that maintain staff, offices, and installations throughout hot spots of the world are advised to adopt comprehensive security programs. Companies like Occidental, Shell, and BP are models of security preparedness; as targets of guerrilla groups in Latin America, they have to be. Security is big business throughout the commercial, industrial, and private sectors in Colombia and elsewhere. The U.S. embassy in Bogota has one of the largest and most effective security programs in the world. Crime and terrorist threats will have to be reduced drastically before tight security can be relaxed.

VARIOUS SCAMS PERPETRATED AGAINST VISITORS

The background report will probably list a sampling of scams that are regularly used against unwitting foreign visitors. For Colombia it would list some of the following true examples:

- Tired travelers arriving at the international airports in Bogota and Cali have been met by criminals posing as local employees. The criminals see a name and a company on a sign held by the genuine greeter, copy it onto their own sign, and move closer to the front of the line. They distract the traveler and take him to their car, where he is abducted, robbed, and sometimes murdered. Visitors should work out a coded signal or parole phrase, like a password phrase, with the greeter to ensure they will be met by the right person.

- Thieves can strike at any time, in tourist areas especially. Not long ago, a visiting U.S. Special Forces soldier taking in the sights near the cable car terminal in Bogota's prime tourist area was dressed in civilian clothes and carrying a backpack. In a matter of seconds, his backpack was slashed from his back and the two robbers got away clean. He was more than a little embarrassed to have to report not only the theft of his backpack, but also the loss of his army-issue 9mm Beretta pistol that was in the backpack.

- A visiting military official, long experienced in Latin American ways, was driving to work one morning, enjoying the beautiful weather. He rolled down the window on the driver's side and placed his elbow on the sill. A young thief sneaked up behind him while he was stopped at a traffic light and yanked his Rolex watch from his wrist. The shocked driver was left sitting in traffic wondering what happened. He bought another Rolex watch and vowed to be more careful, adopting the Colombian habit of wearing it on his right wrist (many Colombian taxi drivers follow this practice). The following month, in the same car at the same intersection, the official was enjoying another rare sunny day on his way to work and he again put his arm out the window. This time he felt a pinprick on his left shoulder and, thinking it was an insect, reached over with his right hand to slap it. Zap, away went his new Rolex. Angrily, but thoughtlessly, he gave chase, racing across traffic on foot after the thief. When a sixth sense told him to look back, he saw another thief driving off with his car. A well-planned operation.

- A Spanish-speaking former U.S. metropolitan police officer working temporarily at the U.S. embassy was stopped on the street outside of a major hotel in downtown Bogota by a man who flashed police identification. The American was asked to show identification and to prove that he had his cash in a safe place. As requested, the man handed his wallet and cash over to the "policeman," who said he could recover the items at the police station in half an hour. The "policeman" gave the American a card with the address and telephone number of the police station and directions on how to get there. Of course, the victim was completely duped, responding naively to the appearance of authority. It was a $2,000 lesson, his entire travel advance, which his parent agency later refused to reimburse.

- A TDY (temporary duty) military officer suffered the same fate a week later, although it only cost him $200.
- A variation of the same scam, in this instance at one of the affluent shopping centers in the north of Bogota, occurred when a car containing three official-looking men who identified themselves as "treasury department" agents demanded to see an American's cash to ensure that it was not counterfeit. The unwitting visitor turned over his cash, accepted a receipt for it, and was given the address of the nearest police station to recover it. Gone! Three such incidents were reported to the U.S. embassy in a two-month period. (Several of the "agents" involved spoke excellent English and were very well mannered.)
- A resident FBI agent in Bogota knew he would be going into a high-crime area, so he took off his prized Rolex and put it in his pocket, a routine precaution. He thought nothing more about it until, just as his business was concluding and he was getting back into his chauffeured official car, he felt a strong hand grasp his bare wrist and then dash off empty handed. A close call.

Armed with this type of precautionary information, available for virtually every country on earth, the businessman is better able to cope with the daily security problems that exist in a particular country. Sometimes, however, more is needed. This is particularly true when corporate foreign investment is involved.

THE RISK ASSESSMENT

We spoke briefly about risk assessments in the first chapter. For a country like Colombia, for example, the full risk assessment would go well beyond the "realities" coverage listed above. It would also cover the political and economic stability of the country and would focus on current trends in threats—especially to foreigners—from the guerrillas and the drug cartels. It would discuss how guerrillas from the National Liberation Army (ELN) and the Colombian Revolutionary Armed Forces (FARC) conduct disruptive operations against Colombian government companies and both the foreign and domestic extractive industries. These operations include extortion of foreign oil companies, kidnap-for-ransom schemes, bombings, and assassinations.

It would warn the pending investor that kidnapping of foreign oil company employees was a growth business, bringing tens of millions of dollars into guerrilla war chests every year, and how extortion operations were bringing millions of dollars a month in payments to the ELN and FARC from the foreign companies involved in the extractive industries alone. It would explain that ineffective and corrupt police forces combined with a justice system in shambles does not auger well for the future.

In short, the entire risk assessment would provide a company with a flashlight to use in that dark Colombian room. It would illuminate the obstacles the company would face if it decided to do business in the country, without making any judgments concerning the desirability of moving ahead. That decision can only be made by the company's management team. The members of that team are the only ones who can weigh the risks against the possible gains. In Colombia, for example, where the picture is clearly not bright, the economy remains strong and many U.S. and other Western companies are making huge profits and are investing heavily in the future of the country. But one thing is certain, all of these successful companies are familiar with the terrain and have adjusted their local operations to deal with the inherent problems as securely and risk free as possible.

THE SPOT REPORT

Occasionally, even companies that are well-versed in the pitfalls of operating within a particular country are faced with unusual circumstances that call for a judgment of a particular situation. This is where the spot report comes in. It's an analysis of a particular situation that may affect a company's operations in a country.

For example, a few years ago an oil company that had been operating successfully in Algeria for many years was suddenly faced with the assassination of the Algerian head of state, Mohammed Boudiaf. The company had worked successfully with the Boudiaf government for a long time and had a number of important contracts and agreements with that old administration. Company officials were poised to visit Algeria to sign a new exploration contract when the assassination took place.

The requirements for the spot report were essentially twofold: (1) provide information concerning the most likely makeup of the new government and an analysis of the likelihood that the new administration would honor contracts and agreements made under the Boudiaf administration; and (2) provide an assessment of the personal risks involved in traveling to Algiers under the current circumstances and whether the Algerian officials they were supposed to meet still had the authority to sign the new contract.

The spot reports that followed (two reports, several days apart) indicated that the situation in Algeria was in a state of uneasy calm, although bands of unruly Islamic fundamentalists supporting the Islamic Salvation Front (FIS) were roaming the streets of Algiers chanting fundamentalist slogans, and isolated gunshots could be heard throughout the day and night. It listed several security incidents that had occurred and cited a State Department advisory that suggested U.S. citizens defer all nonessential travel to Algeria and avoid all public gatherings, demonstrations, and the southern regions of Algeria, if travel was undertaken. It reported that the killer and eleven other Islamic fundamentalists who participated in the well-planned assassination had been killed or captured by the police, and that Defense Minister Khaled Nezzar, the strongman of a four-man leadership, had swiftly appointed Ali Kafti, a prominent war veteran with a reputation for courage and moderation, as Boudiaf's successor.

The reports suggested that the company delay sending its representatives to Algiers until the dust had settled a bit more but stated that the military appeared to have the situation firmly in hand and that any new permanent government would likely be firm in its resolve to keep Islamic fundamentalism from creeping into the government. It opined that all previous contracts and agreements would be honored by the new government, and that the officials the company had been dealing with in the past would be the same ones they would deal with in the future.

The information and analysis contained in the spot reports prevented the oil company from sending its employees into a potentially dangerous situation in the days following the assassination and gave it a level of comfort that its past investments would be secure and that future dealings would be possible on more or less the same grounds as before.

RESEARCH THE LAWS AND CUSTOMS

Never, ever travel to a foreign country without doing at least some basic research about the place. This is particularly true when the country is significantly different culturally from the one in which you are living. Although an American traveling to Europe will see little difference between European cities and people and those found in the United States, this is not the case for many other destinations. Except for minor differences in architecture and some language problems, whether you are in New York, London, Paris, or Frankfurt, things are more or less the same, but when you travel farther afield, say to Africa, Asia, or the Middle East, things can be very, very different. Let's take a look at one that might surprise you.

SAUDI ARABIA

Oil rich Saudi Arabia is a close ally of the United States and the West, and many of its people enjoy Western lifestyles and speak English and other foreign languages. Many Saudis are comfortable living abroad and have attended Western universities and colleges. The Saudis we meet abroad are mostly urbane, are Western educated, and have adapted well to Western cultural mores. But a visit to Jeddah or Riyadh could come as a great shock to the uninformed. Failure to understand the mores and cultural peculiarities of the Saudis in Saudi Arabia can lead to disaster.

Saudi Arabia is a Muslim state, and as such, it treats women differently than we do in the West. Women in Saudi Arabia are not permitted to run around the streets in shorts and halters and can't drive automobiles, for example. This is Saudi law, and violators will be prosecuted or even stoned! Women's rights is not an issue in Saudi Arabia, and indeed in most Muslim countries: they simply don't have any rights.

Parental Abductions

There are many examples of Saudi men who have come to the West for their education and then married Western women and had children born abroad. These children usually have dual nationality, but the foreign (non-Saudi) nationality is not recognized in Saudi Arabia. This is true in most other Muslim countries as well. Saudi Arabia, for example, recognizes only the Saudi nationality, and once inside Saudi Arabia, the children will not be permitted to leave the country without the permission of the Saudi father, despite the wishes of the non-Saudi mother and what should be her rights under international law.

In instances where divorce occurs and the mother is awarded custody of the children in U.S. or Western courts, this custody is simply ignored by most Muslim governments. Therefore, if a Saudi man marries an American woman and they have children and then divorce in the United States, and the woman is awarded primary custody of the children following which he kidnaps the children and takes them to Saudi Arabia, the woman is basically out of luck. Despite the fact that the Saudi government gives lip service to custody laws and the Hague Convention rulings on parental abductions, in fact it will come down on the side of the Saudi father in virtually every case. There are now dozens of cases like this in the courts, but the sad fact is that as long as the children are in the custody of the father in Saudi Arabia, the Saudi government will do nothing to force the return of the children to their foreign mothers. The mother's only recourse is to try to kidnap the children back.

Although internal travel restrictions in Muslim countries make these kinds of operations extremely difficult to pull off, some have been successful. CTC International Group, for example, still holds the record for the most people brought home from an Arab country in a single parental abduction operation: four small children and their American mother were spirited out of The United Arab Emirates (UAE) and the clutches of an abusive Arab father back to the United States. (Unfortunately, the woman failed to follow some basic security precautions after she and her children got back to the United States, and the father kidnapped the children back to the UAE about a year later.)

Travel Restrictions

Saudi Arabia recently relaxed its restrictions on foreign travelers and investors, but the fact remains there is nothing like a tourist visa issued, and in order for a foreigner to receive a visa to visit the country, the individual needs a Saudi sponsor. This often leads to extortion schemes being perpetrated against the foreigners. This is how it works. They are invited to the country to discuss a potentially lucrative business deal. Then, upon arrival in the country, they are ordered to surrender their passports to their Saudi sponsors. But when the visit is over and the visitors want to leave, the sponsors can essentially hold them hostage in Saudi Arabia until they agree to certain terms on a contract or pay the sponsors large sums of money. Even the claim that money is owed to some businessman or merchant is sufficient cause to delay the departure of the foreigner from the country until the alleged debt, true or false, is paid in full.

Even the country's extended royal family gains extra income by using the sponsorship requirement to its advantage. Family members agree to act as sponsors for a fee, which they are certain to collect because of the requirement that the foreigners surrender their passports to the sponsors upon arrival.

Saudi Arabia is considering relaxing its restrictions on foreign investment in order to gain entry in the World Trade Organization (WTO), which has thus far excluded the country because of its prejudicial practices toward non-Saudis. However, the sponsorship issue still hangs over the head of every visitor like the sword of Damocles.

Alcohol and Islam

Another major issue to contend with is alcohol. Drinking alcohol is forbidden under Muslim law, so don't try to bring a bottle of your favorite vodka into the country, and forget about enjoying a bottle of Bordeaux with your meal at the hotel. You can't get a drink, even at the best hotels and restaurants in Saudi Arabia.

With the above said, alcoholic beverages are routinely smuggled into the country and served by Saudis in the privacy of their homes, and many enjoy their scotch when they are free from surveillance outside the country. I used to travel frequently through Jeddah on the Lufthansa flight from Frankfurt to Addis Ababa, Ethiopia, and I never ceased to be amused at the Saudis, particularly the young women, flying in and out of Jeddah. They would board the plane in Jeddah in their traditional caftan robes and veils and sit quietly with their hands in their laps until the plane reached altitude and exited Saudi airspace. Then, as soon as the captain's announcement was heard, a complete transformation would occur.

The women would rush to the rest rooms, where they would change into Western dress and apply their makeup. Then the transformed young women, now clad in miniskirts and tight sweaters, would return to their seats and signal the flight attendant to bring them their first double Johnnie Walker Black on the rocks (or some such concoction) of the flight and settle in for the ride to Frankfurt.

The reverse was true for the Frankfurt-Jeddah return flight. They would board the plane in their fashionable Western garb and enjoy cocktails and wine until the plane neared Saudi airspace. Then the rush for the rest rooms would begin and the women would return to their seats dressed in their caftan robes and sit demurely veiled for the remainder of the flight to Jeddah.

So beware, particularly you ladies, and don't get caught driving a car in your miniskirt while drinking a beer in Jeddah. And if a man looks at you, drop your eyes. You could be subjected to a severe stoning.

A FINAL NOTE

The importance of possessing good, solid business intelligence before entering into any sort of partnership or investment should be abundantly clear by now. Companies that routinely collect information on their business associates before entering into relationships and that keep up to date on what their competitors are doing to grab market share are always going to be better positioned to succeed than those that rely solely on instinct and try to fly by the seat of their pants.

To paraphrase Sun Tzu once again, if you know the weaknesses and capabilities of yourself and your competition and are familiar with the specific environmental culture (the terrain), you cannot fail. The value of thorough, objective intelligence has been recognized since time immemorial. Those who knew this were successful, and those who didn't were doomed to failure. For the life of me, I cannot imagine making any important decision, whether business or personal, without first gathering all of the facts of the case, and then carefully weighing all of those facts before deciding on a course of action. Decisions that are based on solid intelligence and objective analysis are almost always the right ones. (I use the word "almost" because there are some things—acts of God, for example—that can never be anticipated. Luck will always play a role.)

So, whether traveling abroad to unfamiliar countries or dealing with unknown individuals or companies, please don't try to wing it and hope for the best. Do your homework before embarking on any potentially risky venture. Make it a part of your routine. Check people and places out before you jump. Use that flashlight. Illuminate those obstacles. As Sun Tzu advised so long ago: if, after thorough preparation, things don't look just right, at the very least you can decide not to engage.

Appendix:

COMPUTER DATABASES

FREE (OR MOSTLY FREE) INTERNET SITES

Anywho
http://www.anywho.com
Phone numbers, addresses, maps, and directions for businesses and people in the United States.

Worldwide Telephone Searches
http://www.infobel.com/World/

The Ultimate White Pages
http://www.theultimates.com/white/

Search Systems from Pacific Information Services, Inc.
http://www.pac-info.com
Over 4,564 free searchable public records databases

Northern Light
http://www.northernlight.com
Search engine for full text sources

Public Record Finder.com
http://www.publicrecordfinder.com
Search engine designed to locate free public record sites. Over 6,000 links

FedWorld
http://www.fedworld.gov
A comprehensive central access point for searching, locating, ordering, and acquiring government and business information.

FirstGov
http://www.firstgov.gov
Gateway to government information

Corporate Information
http://www.corporateinformation.com

U.S. Securities and Exchange Commission
http://www.sec.gov
Searchable database for filings on public companies. Also has investor information, litigation releases, and regulatory actions.

American Medical Association
http://www.ama-assn.org
Starting place to check out doctors

Martindale-Hubble
http://www.martindale.com
Starting place to check out lawyers

National Association of Securities Dealers
http://www.nasdr.com
Place to check out your broker

Dogpile
http://www.dogpile.com
Meta search engine

Copernic
http://www.copernic.com
Multisearch engine

FEE-BASED OR SUBSCRIPTION INFORMATION SOURCES AND CONTENT PROVIDERS

555-1212
http://www.555-1212.com
Inexpensive telephone lookups

Stat-USA
http://www.stat-usa.com
International market research

Dialog
http://www.dialog.com
Leading e-information and solutions company

DowJones
http://www.dowjones.com
Business and financial news and information

Lexis/Nexis
http://www.lexis-nexis.com
Information for legal, business, academic, and government professionals

Dun & Bradstreet
http://www.dnb.com
Business information reports

Courtlink and Casestream
http://www.courtlink.com
Court records

Electric Library
http://www.elibrary.com
Online research center

Westlaw
http://www.westlaw.com
Research tool for the legal community

FEE-BASED INDIVIDUAL REFERENCE SERVICES

Commercial services that provide data to help identify, verify, or locate individuals or businesses. Usually require a subscription application and permissible use purposes. Customers use these services to detect fraudulent activity, assist law enforcement efforts, locate people and assets, and verify information and identities, as well as many other purposes. Used primarily by insurance companies, law firms, private investigators, and law enforcement and government agencies.

ChoicePoint
http://www.choicepointline.com

Database Technologies
DBT Online
http://www.dbtonline.com

KnowX
http://www.knowx.com

Loc8fast
www.loc8fast.com

Glossary Terms

Access Agent: Intermediary used when direct contact with a potential penetration agent is not possible; agents on the outside who have direct access to people who are on the inside.

Agent: Foreign indigenous spies recruited by an intelligence case officer.

Analysis Unit: The part of an intelligence unit that analyzes and interprets the raw data delivered by the collection unit.

Analytical Approach: A specific process to evaluate a problem and then to come up with a list of possible sources for further inquiry.

Audio Operations: Operations dealing with the collection of audio data; that is, bugging or phone taps.

Backstopped: A story that can be "verified" by a paper trail, false business addresses, phone numbers, and so forth, in order to keep a cover believable when checked out.

Baksheesh: A bribe.

Briefing: A meeting where an agent is told of the task he or she is to undertake.

Business Intelligence: Gathering of data concerning a competing business, industry, market, and so forth.

Case Officer: A covert intelligence officer attached to the operational (clandestine) arm of an intelligence service. The case officer typically is a college graduate, fluent in one or more foreign languages, and always a fully trusted citizen with a top secret security clearance.

Chief of Station (COS): CIA officer in charge of all U.S. clandestine operations within a specific country.

CIA: Central Intelligence Agency. The United States' foreign intelligence and counterintelligence agency.

Clandestine: An operation conducted in secrecy.

Clandestine Tradecraft: Intelligence procedures and techniques.

Collection Unit: The part of the intelligence unit that collects information from human or nonhuman sources and then sends that information back to the analysis unit.

Commo: Abbreviation for communications.

Confidentiality Agreement: A corporate world document that strives to restrict the employee from divulging confidential information and usually includes an acknowledgment from the employee concerning what sort of information is of value to the company and should not be disclosed to other parties.

Counterintelligence: Those actions by an intelligence agency or by a company that are intended to protect their own security and seek out intelligence operations being mounted by others against them.

Cover: The role played by an intelligence officer to conceal his true purpose for living or traveling abroad.

Cover for Action: A case officer's cover as a civilian, foreigner, businessperson, journalist, or any of a wide variety of professions. This cover will usually have an alias, may only be used for a short time, and is backed up with paperwork and personal history.

Cover for Status: The long-term cover that provides the case officer with the legitimacy to work in a particular foreign country.

Covert Methods: Procedures that are performed secretly.

Cryptonym: The name by which agents or intelligence operations are referred to in all correspondence concerning their operational assignments. The first two letters of a cryptonym are a digraph representing the country within which they are operating, and the rest is a word selected more or less at random from the dictionary. In the CIA, cryptonyms are always typed in upper case.

Dangle: Someone placed in the way of a target in an attempt to be picked up and assimilated into the inner ranks. A dangle may be a double agent or someone used in transplant operations.

Database: A collection of organized information.

DCI: Director of Central Intelligence.

Dead Drop: A clandestine hiding place for a message or goods to be retrieved by an agent or case officer at a later time.

Debriefing: The extraction of information from a willing agent that has returned from an intelligence mission.

Defector: A person who leaves their post within a target area and who then shares their secrets in return for compensation and/or asylum. A defector can only provide historical information.

DGSE: Direction Générale de la Sécurité Extérieure. French intelligence and counterinsurgency agency. Formerly SDECE, Service de Documentation Extérieure et Contre-Espionage.

Due Diligence: Background research performed on a person or company that seeks to verify the history or references of the entity before placing trust in it.

Economic Espionage Act (EEA) of 1996: A law enacted to focus attention on the threat of foreign industrial spying and information theft whether it takes place in the United States, on the Internet, or in any international location. It was designed to cover the whole range of trade secrets, which are defined in the act as "information the owner has taken reasonable measures to keep secret," and information that "derives its economic value, actual or potential, from not being generally known to or available to the general public."

Elicitation: Obtaining information directly from a source without asking direct questions as in a debriefing.

Exfiltration: The removal of a person or group of people from an unsafe area.

False Subtraction: A method used in the decoding of encrypted messages.

Farm, The: The CIA's covert training facility in Virginia.

Finished Intelligence: The final product of the intelligence process; it is created after the raw data is analyzed and written in a coherent report.

Flap: An operation that experiences unforeseen problems, usually of a security nature.

GRU: Glavnoe Razvedyvatelnoe Upravlenie. The Soviet military intelligence group and chief intelligence directorate of the Soviet General Staff.

Human Source: A person used to obtain intelligence.
HUMINT: Human intelligence.

IMINT: Imagery intelligence.
Industrial Espionage: Illegal collection of business intelligence.
Information Broker: A source of information, available for a fee.
Information Report: A nonanalyzed report of raw information collected.
In-House Unit: A business intelligence unit that resides within the organization to which it reports.
Intelligence Process: The collection of raw information, analysis of the information, and, finally, the reporting and dissemination of the finished intelligence product to a consumer.
Intelligence Report: The product resulting from the collection, evaluation, analysis, integration, and interpretation of all available information on a subject.
Inter alia: During the course of.
Invention Agreements: A contractual clause whereby any inventions (software, products, and so forth) will remain as the property of the inventor's company.

Legal Traveler: A person who has the ability to travel in and out of a sensitive target country without raising suspicion.
Legend: The in-depth story of a case officer's cover history that the case officer must be able to keep consistent and believable.
Letter Drop: Location used by agents to transfer documents and communiqués. It is usually a post office box or mailing address rented in alias.

MASINT: Measurement and signatures (unique identifiers) intelligence.
MI6: Great Britain's overseas intelligence organization. Also known as the SIS, or Secret Intelligence Service.
Microdots: Photos of messages that are reduced to the size of a period dot and hidden, usually within the text of a cover message.
MSS: The Communist Chinese Ministry of State Security.
Mutually Assured Destruction (MAD): The political belief that if already

nuclear-equipped countries all have the same degree of nuclear technology, no one country will be more powerful than another and a peaceful state will exist.

NCNA: The New China News Agency, Communist China's official news agency.

NOC: Nonofficial covered case officer. This is a case officer whose daily cover (see Cover for Status) may be as a student, businessperson, and so forth rather than as an official of a government.

Noncompetition Agreement: In the corporate world, it strives to prevent an employee from competing with the employer for some specific period of time after termination of employment.

Nondisclosure Agreement: A perpetually binding agreement wherein an employee must not disclose confidential business information during or after employment.

Nonproliferation: A political agreement whereby the countries that did not have nuclear capabilities at the time of signing would not develop them.

NSA: National Security Agency (United States).

One-Way Voice Link (OWVL): The prearranged, regular, shortwave broadcast (usually a reading of sets of numbers) beamed on a specific frequency and meant to be intercepted and decrypted by an agent.

OSS: Office of Strategic Services (United States). The precursor agency to the CIA.

Penetration Agents: Agents recruited because of their status within a target area. The penetration agent is the best type of agent because, once recruited, he or she can provide a continuing stream of current information for as long as he or she is with the target. But he or she is also the most difficult and costly (in terms of time and money) to acquire.

PLA: The Communist Chinese People's Liberation Army.

PRU: Provincial Reconnaissance Unit. Paramilitary CIA units deployed during the Vietnam conflict.

Raindancer: A charlatan technical surveillance countermeasures (TSCM) technician.

Recruitment Cycle: The process of assessing, developing, and recruiting new agents.

Research Source: A source of information on a particular subject.

Risk Analysis: Research that points out the general obstacles to operating securely in a foreign environment.

Safe Haven: A secure place used for clandestine meetings.

Safehouse: A house or apartment that functions as a safe haven for clandestine agent meetings.

Secret Writing (SW): A technique of covert agent communications employing the use of invisible ink or "carbon" paper impregnated with invisible ink.

SIGINT: (Communications) signals intelligence.

SOP: Standard Operating Procedure.

Spot Report: A quick analysis of a particular situation.

Target Analysis: Examination of a target area with an eye toward identifying where within that area the desired information would normally be held (for example, selection of a target department).

Target Area: Area dealt with during an intelligence gathering operation.

Target Department: The section of a target area that contains the desired information or people who have access to that information. Area from which a target individual is selected.

Targeted Collection: Specific information a company can use to increase its productivity or market share. Market analysis, due diligence, background investigations on potential partners, employees and others, and competitor intelligence fall into this category.

Target Individual: A person who has direct knowledge of desired information. The target individual may be found within a target department.

Technical Surveillance Countermeasures (TSCM): Actions, referred to as "sweeps," that are taken to combat technical surveillance such as bugs, wire taps, and so forth.

Tradecraft: The clandestine methods and techniques by which an intelligence agency conducts its covert collection of intelligence.

Trade Secrets: All forms of economically valuable financial, business, scientific, technical, economic, or engineering information that the owner has taken reasonable measures to keep secret.

Uniform Trade Secrets Act: Federal act disallowing, among other things, the transfer of sensitive information among companies by former employees.

Vetted Asset: A human source who has been used before and has been deemed both reliable and trustworthy.

Index

About the Author

F. W. Rustmann Jr. is a twenty-four-year veteran of the CIA's Clandestine Service. He retired in 1990 as a member of the elite Senior Intelligence Service (SIS), with the equivalent rank of major general. He was also an instructor at the CIA's legendary covert training facility, "the Farm." After retiring from the CIA, he founded CTC International Group Limited, a pioneer in the field of business intelligence and a recognized leader in the industry. His numerous articles on business intelligence have appeared in the *Baltimore Sun, Miami Herald, Palm Beach Post,* and elsewhere. He lives in Palm Beach, Florida.